ETHICS
AND ITS
APPLICATIONS

W9-ASE-944

Baruch Brody

Baylor College of Medicine
Rice University

UNDER THE GENERAL EDITORSHIP OF
ROBERT J. FOGELIN,
Dartmouth College

Harcourt Brace Jovanovich, Inc.

New York San Diego Chicago San Francisco Atlanta
London Sydney Toronto

To Jo Monaghan,
whose partnership in producing this book made it possible

ISBN 0-15-524510-4

Library of Congress Catalog Card Number: 82-083246

Printed in the United States of America

Contents

Chapter Five

Chapter Six

Chapter Seven

Chapter Eight

_____ *Chapter Nine* _____

_____ *Chapter Ten* _____

_____ *Chapter Eleven* _____

_____ *Chapter Twelve* _____

_____ *Chapter Thirteen* _____

_____ *Chapter Fourteen* _____

Autonomy and Paternalism: A Deontological Perspective 187

Preface

This book grows out of 15 years' experience in teaching courses on contemporary moral issues, both at MIT and at Rice University. That experience has convinced me that the best way to teach such courses is to examine the implications of important moral theories for significant real-life moral issues. This approach has certainly produced greater student interest. More importantly, it has produced better understanding, because students grasp the meaning of theories much more readily when they are able to see how the theories apply in the real world.

Over the years, I have changed the specific moral issues that I cover to reflect current concerns. But recently I have been emphasizing more perennial problems, even if they are not immediately pressing, as a way of providing greater long-term significance for the course. This book reflects that shift in emphasis. It applies the fundamental moral theories to issues concerning the distribution of wealth, the criminal justice system, life and death choices, and autonomy. These are issues that will continue to be of concern to society, and they deserve emphasis.

My greatest debt is to the many students who have taken this course and who have helped me think these issues through. I have been truly fortunate in having such good students, and I want to thank them. For their help in critiquing earlier versions of this manuscript, I would like to thank Richard T. Garner of Ohio State University, Michael Goldman of Miami University, Hardy Jones of the University of Nebraska at Lincoln, Kenneth Seeskin of Northwestern University, Kathy Shamey of Santa Monica College, K. Sundaram of Lake Michigan College, and Barbara Winters of the University of California at San Diego. Finally, in dedicating this book to Jo, I am merely indicating a debt for all her help, a debt which would be impossible to fully repay.

Baruch Brody
Baylor College of Medicine
Rice University

Introduction

This book is an introduction to a branch of philosophy called ethics. In this opening chapter we will examine the nature of philosophy and ethics, as well as the nature of the ethical concern with contemporary moral issues that this book addresses.

THE NATURE OF PHILOSOPHY

No attempt to define philosophy in some short formula can be very helpful. So, instead, we will begin our inquiry into the nature of philosophy by listing some of the main aspects of philosophical problems and indicating some of the ways in which philosophers try to solve them.

1. Philosophy concerns itself with the nature and validity of various spheres of human life. Every society has its own pattern of social organization. While there are many different patterns, nearly all of them involve an unequal distribution of such resources as wealth, power, prestige, and leisure. Such inequality is normally accepted as an unavoidable fact of life. There are, however, times in which this unequal pattern comes to be challenged, either by those who have few of these resources and want more or by those who have many and are troubled by what they perceive as an unfair distribution. During these times, people ask such questions as, Should society's resources be equally distributed among everyone? If not, by what criteria shall we decide who gets what? In asking these sorts of questions people are challenging the validity of their social structure and seeking ways to improve it. These are philosophical questions and concerns.

Religion is another important sphere of human life which frequently evokes philosophical concerns. Most people are brought up with certain religious beliefs. These beliefs have important implications for the ways in which people should live. In earlier times, religious beliefs were not subject to much question, because nearly everybody in a given society held the same beliefs. This is no longer the case. Our own society, for example, contains a wide variety of religious beliefs and practices as well as many ideologies which omit the religious element altogether. This diversity leads people to ask such questions as, What is the nature of my religious beliefs? Are there any reasons for holding my beliefs rather than some other beliefs? Should religious beliefs make any difference in my life? These, too, are philosophical questions and considerations.

Because all philosophical questions concern the nature and validity of some sphere of human life, there seems to be an area of philosophy devoted to understanding each major aspect of human existence. For example, there is a philosophy of society, a philosophy of religion, a philosophy of art, a philosophy of science, a philosophy of knowledge, and so on. This all-encompassing nature of philosophy explains why it is related to so many other disciplines and why so many people throughout the ages have turned to this field of study for answers to the questions that trouble them.

2. Interest in a particular area of philosophy is usually proportional to the extent to which people feel troubled about the corresponding sphere of human life. Again, the sphere of religion will serve to illustrate the point. In times of tranquility, religious people usually do not question their beliefs or the life that their beliefs presuppose. They have very little real interest in the philosophy of religion during these periods, except perhaps as an abstract, intellectual game. But in times of upheaval or despair, religious people tend to become troubled about their beliefs and about what implications these beliefs have for people's lives. During the Middle Ages, for instance, the rise of interest in Aristotelian philosophy and Greek science posed a severe intellectual challenge to the religious beliefs then commonly held. Not surprisingly, the Middle Ages was one of the golden periods in the philosophy of religion. Our present era is another such period. The rise of an increasingly secular world view associated with the growth of modern science has posed a severe challenge to traditional religious beliefs. And it is not surprising that the philosophy of religion is currently a flourishing area of investigation.

Similarly, during times of economic prosperity and social harmony, few people question the unequal distribution of society's resources, and inquiries into the nature of justice and of what makes a just society are primarily abstract, intellectual issues about which most people have very little interest. But in different times, social forces rise to challenge this previously accepted unequal distribution of resources. Our own era is such a time, and it is not surprising that interest in the philosophy of society has increased greatly in recent years.

3. Philosophical investigation into a sphere of human life can cause us to greatly change the ways we behave within that sphere. Any philosophical examination into the nature and validity of a major sphere of human life may produce a negative view of the normal pattern of activities within that sphere of life. Such a negative evaluation has the potential to be revolutionary in that it can lead to substantial changes. For this reason, philosophy has always been viewed with a certain amount of suspicion by defenders of the status quo. Indeed, one of the world's first great philosophers, Socrates, was sentenced to death for his philosophical activities, which many of his fellow Athenians felt were corrupting the young. Even when philosophical examination supports the validity of normal activities within a given sphere of human life, the investigation can still have a great impact by strengthening that dimension of life.

Examples from the sphere of religion will illustrate this point. One of the great Greek philosophers, Plato, in a dialogue called the *Euthyphro*, called into question the validity of the then-common Greek religious view that if man gives God what God wants and needs then God will give man what man wants and needs. Plato pointed out that this conception of religion as a trade was incompatible with our understanding that an all-perfect God did not need anything which man could provide. This philosophical challenge had a revolutionary impact on subsequent thinking about the man-God relationship. On the other hand, St. Thomas Aquinas, the great medieval Catholic philosopher, did not have this type of revolutionary impact. This is not surprising, since the results of his investigation reaffirmed the validity of the beliefs and practices of his religious community rather than challenged them. Nevertheless, his philosophical activity did have a profound impact on the *practice* of religion by strengthening it and by giving believers a deeper understanding of the content of their faith.

To summarize, philosophical investigation into a sphere of human activity can make a tremendous difference in the way people behave within that sphere. It may strengthen our commitment to current beliefs and practices, or it may lead to revolutionary changes.

4. Philosophers are concerned with finding answers that can be rationally defended.   Consider, for example, the question, Is there a God? This is a typical philosophical question, for it probes the validity of a belief that is fundamental to the sphere under investigation, in this case to many religious traditions. There are only two possible answers to this question, yes and no. What, then, can the philosopher contribute to a discussion of this question? What gives the philosophical treatment of this question the potential to have a powerful impact?

The answer to these questions is very straightforward. Philosophers are not concerned merely with finding answers to their questions; they are concerned with finding answers that can be defended by rational argumentation. This means that philosophers need to think up reasons to support their answers. Many people attempt to answer philosophical questions: some base their answers on personal feelings, some on social traditions, and so on. But we have no reason to be moved by these sorts of answers. What distinguishes the philosophical approach is that it attempts to answer philosophical questions by an appeal to reason. When the philosopher succeeds—that is, when he gives us rational reasons for accepting his answer—then we are moved. When Plato argued against the conventional view of religion, the Greeks, and those who followed them, were moved to transform their religious beliefs, because they saw (and those who came after agreed) that Plato had given good reasons for rejecting that conception of religion. When St. Thomas claimed that God exists, people were moved by his claim, because he offered a rationally defensible argument to back it up.

The sphere of religion has provided us with our illustrative examples. But these examples can be generalized to explain and defend our point that philosophy has the impact it does on *all* spheres of human life because the philosopher backs up his answers to philosophical questions with sound reasons, not merely with beliefs, intuitions, or traditions.

With this brief introduction to the nature of philosophy, we can now apply these four points to the particular area of philosophy we will by studying in this book, ethics.

THE NATURE OF THEORETICAL ETHICS

Ethics is the branch of philosophy that deals with the moral dimension of human life. Therefore, it follows from our preceding account of the nature of philosophy that (1) ethics concerns itself with the nature and validity of the moral dimension of human life; (2) that interest in ethics is usually proportional to the extent to which people feel troubled about the moral dimension of their lives; (3) that ethical investigations can make a great difference to our moral behavior; and (4) that this impact is possible because ethicists can respond to their philosophical questions with rationally defensible answers. In this section we will focus on the nature of ethics, looking at how philosophers analyze the nature and validity of the moral dimension of human life. In the next section, which will make the transition from this Introduction to Chapter 1 of the text, we will explore the three other characteristics of ethics.

The moral dimension of human life seems to presuppose the following three points:

1. There is a real and important difference between actions which are right and actions which are wrong.
2. In many cases, we have the capacity to know, or at least to have justified beliefs about, which actions are right and which actions are wrong. However, there may well be cases in which, at least for the moment, we can only guess.

3. This knowledge (or justified belief) of what is right and what is wrong can have an impact on our behavior. Specifically, we are sometimes led to do an action solely because we come to know (or to be justified in believing) that it is the right thing to do. Similarly, we are sometimes led *not* to do an action solely because we come to know (or to be justified in believing) that it would be the wrong thing to do.

Let us see why the moral dimension of human life presupposes all these beliefs.

The moral sphere of our lives is heavily structured around our beliefs concerning the rightness and wrongness of a variety of actions. Now, suppose that there is no real difference between actions which are right and actions which are wrong. Then all our moral beliefs, which presuppose that there is this difference, would be inappropriate and there would be little which is valid left to the moral dimension of human existence. Or, suppose that there *is* a difference between actions which are right and actions which are wrong, but that the difference is unimportant and of trivial consequence. Then our moral beliefs might be true or false, but they would have no significance and there would be little of value left to the moral dimension of human existence. The moral sphere of life presupposes, therefore, that there is a real and important difference between actions which are right and actions which are wrong.

The second presupposition is that we can sometimes know (or at least have justified beliefs as to) which actions are right and which actions are wrong. Suppose that this were not so. Suppose, instead, that we agree that there is a real and important difference between right and wrong actions but insist that humans can never know which actions are right and which wrong, and, further, that we can never even be justified in believing that certain actions are right and others wrong. Suppose, in other words, that all we have are guesses about what is right and what is wrong. This supposition would go a long way toward undercutting the validity of the moral dimension of human existence. In trying to act morally, we would only be guessing as to what morality requires of us, and we would have no serious reasons on which to base those guesses. Therefore, if we are to take morality seriously, we must presuppose that human beings do have the capacity either to know which actions are right and which are wrong or at least to be justified in their beliefs as to which are right and which wrong.

The third presupposition of the moral dimension of human existence is that this knowledge (or justified belief) about what is right and what is wrong can have an impact on our behavior. In particular, we are sometimes led to do an action solely because we come to know (or to be justified in believing) that it is the right thing to do. Similarly, we are sometimes led *not* to do an action solely because we come to know (or to be justified in believing) that it is the wrong thing to do. But suppose that this is not the case. Suppose that our knowledge of (or our justified belief about) what is right and what is wrong can never have any impact on the way we behave. This supposition would greatly undercut the validity of the moral dimension of human existence, for if our moral knowledge (or our justified moral beliefs) cannot affect the way we behave, it cannot have the impact we all expect it to have. For this reason, the moral dimension of human existence presupposes that this knowledge (or justified belief) about what is right and what is wrong can have an impact on our behavior.

Not all ethicists have been willing to accept these presuppositions. Some, called ethical nihilists, deny that there is any difference between right and wrong actions. Others, called ethical subjectivists, say that there is no significant difference between what is right and what is wrong, because what makes an action right is my (or my society's) approval of that action while what makes an action wrong is my (or my society's) disapproval of the action. There are also moral skeptics, people who deny the possibility of knowing (or even of having justified beliefs as to) which actions are right and which actions are wrong. Finally, there are those who claim that factors in our background, independent of our moral knowledge, lead us to behave the way we do and that our moral knowledge can have no causal significance.

Theoretical ethics is concerned with critically evaluating the foregoing presuppositions of the moral dimension of human existence in light of these theories which challenge those presuppositions. This book, however, is not about theoretical ethics. Therefore, we will accept the presuppositions of the moral sphere of life and go on to deal with the ethical problems described in the next section. In accepting these presuppositions, we are not suggesting that the concerns of theoretical ethics are uninteresting or easily dismissible. Indeed, these are difficult and fascinating questions which the reader is urged to study. We skip over them simply because they are not relevant to our discussion. Rather, this book is grounded in a different area of philosophical investigation, called *applied ethics*. Next, we will examine the concerns of this field of study in general and of this book in particular.

THE NATURE OF APPLIED ETHICS

We saw in the last section that theoretical ethics concerns itself with the nature and validity of the moral dimension of human life. In this section, we shall develop more fully the ideas that (1) interest in ethics is usually proportional to the extent to which people feel troubled about the moral dimension of their lives; (2) that ethical investigations can make a great difference to our moral behavior; and (3) that this impact is possible because ethicists can respond to their philosophical questions with rationally defensible answers. We shall see how these points, in the contemporary context, lead us directly to the study of applied ethics.

Why might people be troubled about the nature and validity of the moral sphere of their lives? Sometimes they are troubled by information which challenges one or more of their fundamental ethical beliefs or the life that those beliefs presuppose. For instance, a person who has grown up in an environment in which everyone shares the same ethical views may come to be troubled about morality upon his first exposure to people who express very different moral views. He may, for example, start to wonder whether there is in fact a difference between right and wrong, or whether, if there is a difference, we can ever really know what is right and what is wrong. This is one type of experience that can lead people to be troubled about the theoretical foundations of the moral dimension of their lives; but it is not terribly likely to be the cause of unease in most modern societies.

It seems, rather, that many people today are troubled about the moral sphere of human life because they do not see how to properly apply their beliefs to many of the ongoing moral questions which our society confronts. The type of ethics with which this book is concerned, applied ethics, is an attempt to respond to this problem. Specifically, this book presents a philosophical investigation of several important issues within the moral sphere of life in contemporary American society. These moral issues arise out of the following observations.

1. Our new technology has given rise to new moral problems. One good example of this, and one of our major subjects of analysis, stems from the ability of medical science to artificially prolong people's lives. This technology forces us to confront several disturbing questions: When does life end? When *should* life end? Should people be allowed to refuse life-saving medical treatment? These are only some of the questions that advances in medical technology now force us to confront — questions that many people find troubling because they do not see how their ethical beliefs can answer them.

2. Some of our familiar institutions do not seem to be working as well as they did in the past. A good example of this, and one which constitutes another major subject of our analysis, is the criminal justice system. There seems to be a growing sense that our criminal justice system is failing to control crime in America. At the same time, there appears to be an increasing sense that many of our familiar practices in the area of criminal justice are inappropriate and unconstitutional because they violate criminals' rights. These observations lead people to think about such questions as, What is the goal of the criminal justice system? Is it to deter crime, to seek retribution, or what? What are the permissible techniques we can use to successfully implement the desired goal? Do we need to find alternatives to our present system? Here, too, many people are troubled because they do not see how their ethical theories can respond to these questions.

3. Old absolutes are now seen as being in need of modifications and exceptions. A good example of this is our current system of taxation and welfare, another of our major subjects of analysis. Not many years ago, hardly anyone questioned whether a just society, like the one we aspire to have in America, should take care of the needs of all its citizens while still allowing those who work to reap the benefits of their labor. But recent economic developments have complicated matters so that it is now difficult to see how these values can simultaneously be achieved. Satisfaction of the absolute value of justice demands increasingly more social welfare benefits, while satisfaction of the absolute value of rewarding people's efforts requires ever lower taxes. Our inability to accommodate both these values forces us to reevaluate our old solutions, and we are troubled because our moral theories do not seem to help us resolve the dilemma.

These examples, and many others which can be given, illustrate that contemporary society is troubled about the moral dimension of human life. We are confronting many practical moral problems which our theoretical moral beliefs seem unable to resolve. These problems are not challenges to the validity of the moral dimension of our lives. They do not suggest that there is no difference between right and wrong or that we have no way of ever knowing what is right and what is wrong. What these problems do suggest is that we are having great difficulty applying our ethical knowledge to many of the practical issues we are now confronting.

Applied ethics is an attempt to respond to these problems by developing philosophical theories that have specific implications for specific moral issues. People turn to applied ethics for solutions to these problems when they seek answers which, because they can be rationally justified, can and should have an impact on their moral behavior.

We begin our introduction to applied ethics with a presentation of two radically conflicting moral theories. These theories were originally developed by theoretical ethicists who put them forward as responses to questions concerning the nature and validity of the moral dimension of human life. But we will use them for more than that, applying them to many of the value problems currently facing our society.

Chapter One

Consequentialism

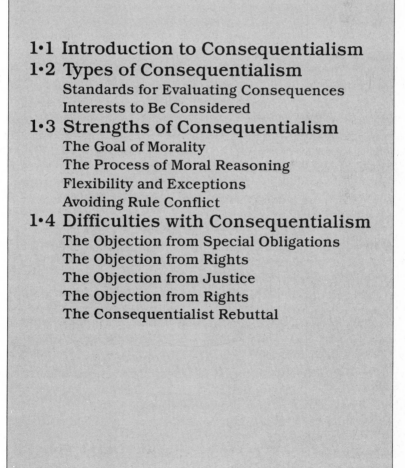

1·1 INTRODUCTION TO CONSEQUENTIALISM

The first approach to resolving moral issues we will consider is one commonly known as *consequentialism.* The basic thesis of this approach is that the rightness or wrongness of an action is based solely on the consequences of performing it; the right action is that which leads to the best consequences. Although this thesis may seem simplistic and obviously true, we shall see in a moment that the basic formulation is both highly ambiguous and controversial.

How do consequentialists go about deciding what is the right thing to do in a given situation? First, they seek to determine all the available alternatives. Next, from a list of these alternatives, they try to foresee the consequences of performing each of them. Finally, they evaluate the consequences in terms of which is best. The action that is most likely to have the best consequences is the one judged to be the right thing to do. To illustrate, let's look at a classic example of a moral dilemma.

In 1841, the *William Brown,* a ship sailing from Liverpool to Philadelphia, struck an iceberg and sank. Two lifeboats, neither very safe, were lowered and then became separated. One was so overloaded with passengers it was barely able to move. It began to leak and then a squall came up. The captain realized that unless the load was lightened everyone might die, but since no one volunteered to jump overboard, he was faced with a moral dilemma. What should he do?

As a consequentialist, the first thing the captain must do is consider the alternatives open to him. One, of course, is to do nothing and hope the lifeboat will not capsize. Another is to encourage volunteers to sacrifice themselves but not to force anyone overboard. And a third alternative is to force some people overboard. This last choice will have several versions, depending upon what process is adopted for deciding who should be thrown overboard. Given these alternatives, the captain then has to determine the likely consequences of each of them. The probable outcome of the first action (doing nothing) is that the boat will capsize and everyone will die. Still, the captain must take into account the possibility that this will *not* happen. The likely consequence of the second alternative (encouraging volunteers) will depend upon the people involved, the effectiveness of the encouragement, and so forth. For the third option, the likely consequence is that those thrown overboard will die and that the rest will be saved.

Ingenuity is required to make sure that one has really considered all the feasible alternatives. And in calculating the consequences, one always has to allow for uncertainty. Thus, the decision maker must be satisfied with statistical probabilities rather than known facts. For example, the captain does not know for sure that the boat will capsize if everyone stays on board. Nor can he be certain that the boat will not capsize anyway; or, even if it does not, that those who remain will be rescued. Finally, in weighing the consequences, he must deal with the question of what is the best consequence, since a good consequence for some may be a bad consequence for others. Pushing some people overboard may be good for those who remain, but clearly it is not so good for those who get pushed. How is one to weigh the gains for some against the losses for others?

We will look more closely at these issues and at others involving the definition of consequentialism in a short while. For now, however, it is important to stop and look at three crucial points concerning the discussion thus far.

1. In the minds of many people, any version of the third alternative is wrong. These individuals argue that to force some people off the lifeboat is to kill them, and that murder is wrong, no matter what the consequences. Those who would say this are appealing to a very different approach to thinking about moral issues. They are saying that certain actions are intrinsically wrong and should not be performed even if the consequences are desirable. Consequentialists reject this alternative way of thinking about moral issues. For them, actions hold no intrinsic value; whether they are right or wrong depends solely upon their consequences in a given situation.

2. A certain type of action may have quite desirable consequences in some situations but not very desirable consequences in others. For example, forcing some people off the boat, if in fact that is the only way to prevent everyone from dying, may on the whole have good consequences *in this situation.* But in most situations, forcing people off a boat and leaving them to drown has very bad consequences on the whole. So, if the rightness and wrongness of an action is to be determined by the consequences, then the same type of action may be right in one situation and wrong in another. In this respect, consequentialism may properly be described as a form of *situation ethics,* an approach to moral issues based on the view that the moral quality of an action varies from one situation to another.

3. In any given situation, an action can be viewed as a means toward attaining certain consequences, and the consequences can be viewed as the ends obtained. For instance, if the captain forces some people off the boat, he is adopting that extreme course of action as a means toward obtaining certain desired results, namely, saving the lives of other people; and this result is the end he is seeking. If, therefore, one is a consequentialist, then one is com-

mitted to a view that the ends (the consequences) justify the means (the actions).

It is obvious that the second and third implications of consequentialism follow from the first. Thus, consequentialists, by saying that actions are neither intrinsically right nor wrong but that, instead, their rightness or wrongness depends on their consequences, are committed to the views that the ends justify the means and that the rightness or wrongness of an action varies from one situation to another.

These implications help bring out the controversial nature of the consequentialist approach. Most traditional Western systems of morality are based on the idea that certain actions are intrinsically right or wrong, and if they are wrong, they should not be adopted as means, even to attain the finest ends. Thus, the Sixth Commandment—Thou shalt not commit murder—does not mean that murders should not be committed in situations in which murders lead to bad results but that they may be committed in situations in which murders lead to good results. At the least, it means that, except in very special circumstances, murders should not be committed, no matter how much good can be produced. Therefore, those who believe in the Ten Commandments, or in any of the wide variety of traditional moral commands and prohibitions concerning ethical conduct, cannot accept the consequentialist approach to moral issues. Similarly, those who are consequentialists must reject the tacit assumption of most traditional morality, that there are actions which are intrinsically right or wrong. Consequentialism is, therefore, a highly revolutionary and controversial challenge to traditional morality.

In the next section we look more carefully at what the consequentialists are saying, and following that we examine the arguments given in support of the consequentialist approach.

1·2 TYPES OF CONSEQUENTIALISM

We have seen that the fundamental thesis of consequentialism is that the right action in given circumstances is the one which will lead to the best consequences for those circumstances. By looking at this proposition more closely, we can see that there are two fundamental ambiguities that must be cleared up before we can use this thesis in thinking about the many contemporary issues with which we will be concerned in this book. First, by what standards are we to decide that one set of consequences is better than another? And second, whose interests shall we take into account when we evaluate the consequences? Different proponents of consequentialism answer these questions differently.

Standards for Evaluating Consequences

The classic account of the standards for evaluating consequences is the thesis of *hedonism*, the belief that the best consequences are the most pleasurable consequences. Put another way, the hedonist thesis is that the presence of pleasure and the absence of pain constitute the standards for evaluating the consequences of our actions. In short, pleasure is the good which morality aims to produce.

At first glance, the hedonist thesis seems implausible. After all, there are so many other conditions (such as health, love, truth, beauty, knowledge) that seem to be good. Why should we judge the consequences of actions just in terms of the pleasure involved in them and not because they lead to more love or to better health or to more knowledge?

Hedonists dismiss this objection on the grounds that it rests upon a misunderstanding of their thesis. They argue that pleasure is simply the *ultimate* standard for judging the consequences of actions, and that all these other conditions are good because they lead to pleasure. In this regard, good health is a source of great pleasure, as is the experience of love, the finding of beauty, and so on. The hedonist, therefore, agrees that these other things are good, but only because they lead to pleasure. If they did not lead to pleasure, they would be worthless. Thus, a certain action may result in the production of something beautiful, but if no one ever sees it (so no one ever gets any pleasure from it), the mere existence of this beautiful creation is itself of no value. In short, then, the hedonist believes that pleasure is the one and only ultimate standard for judging the value of consequences.

Not all consequentialists, however, are hedonists. To understand the nonhedonist argument, we must keep in mind the connection between pleasure and the satisfaction of desires. Normally, we feel pleasure only when (a) some desire is satisfied and (b) we are aware that this desire is satisfied. So, in effect, the hedonist is saying that the ultimate standard for judging the consequences of actions is the awareness of satisifed desires. Nonhedonistic consequentialists are divided into two camps on the basis of their objections to this thesis. The first group claims that hedonists are wrong because consequences that lead to the satisfaction of some desire may be valuable even if we are not aware that the desire is being satisfied. The second group claims that hedonists are wrong because there are some instances in which the satisfaction of some desire is not valuable, even when we are aware that the desire is satisfied. Two examples will help clarify these alternative viewpoints.

Death-Bed Promises.   Suppose you promise a friend on his death bed that you will take care of a vase he has long cherished. The friend dies. Is keeping your promise the right thing to do? Suppose you don't really care about the vase and about whether the promise is kept. Caring for the vase cannot be the right thing to do, because it does not give you any pleasure and your friend is not around to get any pleasure. Nevertheless, many people feel that the morally right thing to do is to keep this promise. How can this be explained on consequentialist grounds? Hedonists seem to offer no answer. We may, however, say the following. If your friend cared for this vase, then his desire will be satisfied, even though he is dead and will not be aware of having his desire satisfied. The action is the right thing to do because it satisfies desires even if it brings no pleasure. Hedonism is incorrect because it insists that the person who had the desire must be aware of, and therefore take pleasure from, the satisfaction of the desire. Therefore, consequentialists should reject hedonism and adopt the view that the standard for judging consequences is the satisfaction of desires.

Sadists and Masochists.   Suppose Mary is a sadist and derives a great deal of pleasure from beating people up, and suppose Joe is a masochist who receives pleasure from being beaten up. Shall we say that it is right for Mary to beat Joe because the consequence of such an action is pleasure for both parties? Many would say no. They would argue that only the satisfaction of *some* desires is valuable. The satisfaction of other desires, desires which are in one way or another unacceptable, is not valuable. According to this approach, what is wrong with hedonism is that it counts the satisfaction of all desires, as long as we are aware that they are satisfied; not just some desires.

It is clear, therefore, that there are a number of standards consequentialists can use for evaluating the results of actions. They can look at the pleasure which results from these actions, at the desire-satisfaction which results from these actions, or at the satisfaction of the "proper" desires which result from these actions. Although historically most consequentialists have been hedonists, the majority of consequentialists today seem to prefer the second view, that the standard for evaluating consequences is the resulting satisfaction of desires. This is the version of consequentialism we will employ throughout the book. At several points, however, we will show how the adoption of a different answer may have important implications.

Interests to Be Considered

One classic answer to the question of whose interests to consider when deciding which action to perform is that one should choose the action which produces the best consequences for oneself. This is the thesis of *egoism*.

Egoists do not suggest that we totally disregard the implications of our actions for other people. For one thing, we can often benefit when good things happen to others; for instance, we indirectly benefit when those whom we love and care about (family, friends) do well. Therefore, in many cases the right thing to do is to help the people we love. In other cases, if we aid people, they will come to our aid in return. In these cases the rational egoist will do what is best for other people so that he will gain in the long run. In essence, then, the egoist says that the right action is the one that will lead to the best consequences for himself in the long run, and that may often mean sacrificing his short-run interests so that others may immediately gain.

This thesis of egoism has been rejected by most consequentialists. Their view is that egoism may be a sound account of rational self-interest but that it is not a sound account of morality. Morality, they maintain, involves counting the consequences for others and not merely for oneself.

This nonegoist approach claims that we must take into account the consequences for all those affected by the action. Thus, an action is right if it leads to the best consequences in terms of the gains and losses to everyone. This version of consequentialism, known as *altruism*, is the one that we will employ throughout the rest of this book. Let us, then, address some of the difficulties inherent in this approach. To begin with, what do we mean when we say "all those affected"? Are we referring only to human beings already born? Would we count fetuses? Would we count future generations not yet born? Would we count conscious animals? Would we count nature itself? These questions, and the answers we give to them, have profound implications for many of the issues we will discuss in this book. Second, once we determine who is affected, how are we to compare the gains of some and the losses of others? Can we meaningfully say that an action is right because the satisfaction of desires that it leads to for some people outweighs the frustration of desires that it leads to for others?

We have considered a number of versions of consequentialism. The one that we will use in this book is that an action is right if, in a given situation, it leads to a greater satisfaction of desires, taking into account all those affected, than does any other available alternative. We call this nonhedonist version of altruistic consequentialism *utilitarianism*.

1·3 STRENGTHS OF CONSEQUENTIALISM

Consequentialism, while a highly controversial thesis, has nevertheless found many supporters for whom its strengths outweigh its controversial nature. Proponents of this approach generally point to four major strengths of consequentialism.

The Goal of Morality

One of the difficult questions that any moral theory has to answer is, Why are moral actions so praiseworthy? Our moral instincts seem to tell us that morality is an extremely serious dimension of life, and that we all have a great stake in seeing to it that the right action is performed. Consequentialism is in a very good position to explain why we hold this view, for it states that morality is not simply obedience to a series of rules whose point is unclear but that moral actions lead to the fulfillment of our desires. It is because moral actions promote this worthwhile goal that we view them so favorably.

It is important to be clear about this point. Consequentialism does not have (and no theory has) a simple answer to the question, Why should I be moral? Only egoists, for whom morality equals rational self-interest, have a simple answer. What consequentialism does have is an answer to the question of the *importance* of morality. It asserts that morality is important because the performance of right actions leads to the general satisfaction of human desires.

The Process of Moral Reasoning

All of us must frequently confront moral choices, and many times we are relatively clear as to which is the right course of action. Other times, however, we do not have that surety. The captain of the lifeboat, for instance, was rightfully unsure as to what he ought to do. And while that example is obviously more dramatic than situations we normally face, it is representative of a circumstance in which moral decision making is extremely difficult. In some cases we may even be unclear as to how to go about discovering what is the right thing to do.

Herein lies another appeal of consequentialism. The consequentialist at least offers a relatively clear procedure for finding out what is the right thing to do: list the alternatives, ascertain their probable consequences, and evaluate the consequences in light of their implications for everyone affected. Clearly, each of these steps involves many problems, and in most cases it is not easy to be sure that one has carried out all those steps adequately. Still, one at least has some guidelines. And in this respect, consequentialism seems to have an advantage as a moral theory.

Flexibility and Exceptions

We have said that much of traditional morality consists of a wide variety of rules telling us what we ought to do and what we should not do. Most consequentialists, and most people in general, would agree that many of these rules are sound. In most cases, the right thing to do is to follow the rules. But even the most ardent adherents to rules agree that there are special cases in which the right thing to do is to disregard the rules.

Consider, as an extreme example, the moral prohibition against torture. There are few people of sound moral judgment who would quarrel with this rule in general. Nevertheless, even here exceptions can be made. Consider the classic example of a terrorist who has planted a bomb which will shortly go off and kill many thousands of people. The police catch the terrorist, but he refuses to tell them where the bomb is planted. If by torturing the terrorist, the police can discover the location of the bomb in time to defuse it or to evacuate the area, would they be right to choose this course of action? Reluctant as we are to adopt such methods, how can we refuse to do so when thousands of lives are at stake?

Consequentialism seems to offer us a way out of this sort of dilemma by regarding plausible moral rules as useful rules of thumb rather than as inviolate commandments. Experience has taught us that, in most cases, following these rules will lead to the best consequences. However, when the circumstances are unusual and an examination of the consequences leads to the conclusion that the best results will come from breaking the moral rule, then we must treat the case as an exception. The consequentialist, then, would see the bomb-threat situation as an unusual circumstance with special consequences and would suspend the rule-of-thumb prohibition against torture in order to achieve the best result — saving thousands of lives.

In short, then, consequentialists claim that morality is more flexible than it traditionally has been viewed, and that their approach to resolving moral dilemmas provides a key to mobilizing this flexibility. We simply need to recognize the special cases in which there is good reason to believe that the consequences of following the traditional moral rule are worse than the consequences of making an exception.

Avoiding Rule Conflict

One of the most difficult moral problems is that in which two rules come into conflict. In such cases, each of the rules seems plausible and yet there is no way to follow the demands of both. A current debate over an aspect of criminal law provides a good example of this conflict.

In some instances, the right of a newspaper to gather and to print information about an accused criminal may interfere with the right of the accused individual to a fair trial. In such cases, should the judge bar publication of this material? On the one hand, we accept the rule that accused criminals should not be deprived of their right to a fair trial. On the other hand, we also accept the rule that a free press should be allowed to publish information that it judges to be of public interest. The first rule seems to dictate that the judge prohibit publication of certain information, while the second rule seems to admonish him to do nothing to prevent its publication. Which course should he follow?

Consequentialists do not claim to have an easy answer to this question. They do claim, however, that they can provide us with a vehicle for helping to resolve such conflicts. From the consequentialist perspective, the existence of a conflict in rules is a signal that we are dealing with one of those exceptional circumstances in which we cannot simply follow even the soundest of rules. The consequentialist, therefore, advises the judge to examine the consequences of each of the options open to him and to choose the action with the best consequences. Here, the strength of the consequentialist approach is that it points out those cases in which one cannot rely upon traditional moral rules.

In putting forward these merits of consequentialism, proponents are not claiming to offer us an easy way out of moral conflicts or dilemmas. They are simply asserting that their theory can help demystify morality by providing a rational methodology for dealing with moral issues. And it is this reasonable claim that, ultimately, is the attraction of consequentialism.

1·4 DIFFICULTIES WITH CONSEQUENTIALISM

There are many moral theorists who argue that consequentialism has to be rejected. We will examine the different reasons for this claim shortly, but first it should be noted that all these reasons turn on the premise that consequentialism presents a much too monolithic view of morality. Let's see what this means.

The consequentialist argues that the *sole* criterion to be used in evaluating actions is the consequences of those actions for all who are involved. Now, while few would deny that the consequences for those affected by an action must certainly be taken into account when evaluating that action, critics of consequentialism argue that there are *many* factors that must be considered, and consequentialism must be rejected because it is only willing to consider one of them.

With this basic argument against consequentialism in mind, let's look now at the different objections to it.

The Objection from Special Obligations

Suppose you are faced with a choice between two actions—one will benefit your family, the other will benefit strangers. Suppose, moreover, that the benefit to the strangers is greater than the benefit to your family. It seems to follow, by the consequentialist criterion, that the right action is the one that will benefit the strangers. Conceivably, there could be times when the benefit to strangers would so outweigh the benefit to family that this implication of consequentialism would be acceptable. In ordinary circumstances, however, anticonsequentialists argue that you should do the action that is beneficial to your family, not the one that benefits the strangers.

The point of this example is to illustrate a major objection to consequentialism—that it does not account for the fact that we have special obligations to certain people, such as family and friends, individuals to whom we have made promises, those who have helped us in the past and to whom we are grateful, and so on. These special obligations, it seems, often require us to put the interests of these special people before the interests of strangers. Consequentialism, however, would have us weigh the interests of everyone equally. So this first objection is that consequentialism is inadequate as a moral theory because it fails to take into account our special moral obligations to people with whom we have a special relation.

The Objection from Rights

Suppose you own a piece of property. Normally, the rights of ownership say that other people cannot use your property without your permission. There will be many cases, however, in which other people can use that property in such a way that the benefits to them and to society in general may be far greater than the benefits you derive from using your property. According to consequentialism, it follows that in all such cases it is morally correct for the other people to use your property even without your permission. This judgment seems to go counter to our normal feelings about this matter, for most people believe that everyone has a right to control the use of his own property, except when a social need is so pressing as to outweigh the individual right.

The second objection, then, is that consequentialism does not take into account the existence of individual rights in deciding on moral issues. Similar examples would include any situation involving the right to life, the right to bodily integrity, the right to privacy, and so forth. The traditional morality supports the view that, generally, others may not infringe upon an individual's rights, even when some social gain could be realized from such infringement. Consequentialism, because it fails to make provisions for individual rights, is unable to do justice to this aspect of morality.

The Objection from Justice

We confer awards and mete out punishments in accordance with our ideas of justice. Rewards should go to those who have earned them in proportion to the extent to which they have been earned; punishments should go to those who deserve them in proportion to the extent to which they are deserved. These views represent some of our most fundamental intuitions about justice, and when these rules are violated, we feel that something very wrong has been done. Consider the familiar example of a teacher who punishes the whole class when only some of the students have misbehaved. Those who are innocent of any wrongdoing often become indignant at being unjustly and wrongly punished. And the guilty, because they are punished no more than the others, have essentially gotten away with their misdeed. When this form of punishment is used on a larger basis, such as when an occupying power punishes a whole civilian population for the acts of a few terrorists, we believe that a great injustice has been done.

These sorts of feelings about justice can, however, pose a serious problem for consequentialism. It is not hard to imagine cases in which the use of something like collective punishment could produce beneficial results. Do we want to say that it would be right to punish collectively in order to get these results? And if we do not, can we accept consequentialism? Again, by only paying attention to one factor, the consequentialist has left out other important moral factors, such as justice, that need to be weighed.

The Consequentialist Rebuttal

Consequentialists are well aware of these objections, and in trying to meet them, they have adopted one of two strategies. First, there are those who accept the implications that consequentialism responds inadequately to traditional morality. But, they argue, since our normal consciousness is the result of incorrect moral reflection and training, its views should be rejected whenever they conflict with the views of consequentialism. The second consequentialist strategy is to suggest that these seeming conflicts between consequentialism and normal moral consciousness can be resolved by fully considering all consequences of the actions. This group proposes that disregard of special moral obligations, violation of individual rights, and inattention to justice have subtle consequences of a very harmful nature. And were these consequences adequately considered, the apparent conflict between consequentialism and traditional morality would disappear.

In this chapter we have laid out some of the strengths and weaknesses of consequentialism. But there is no need to make up your mind now as to whether the consequentialist is right. In a way, the rest of this book is designed to help you do that. Only after we have fully explored the implications of consequentialism for many concrete questions will you have enough information to be in a position to make up your mind. In the next chapter we examine the major alternative approach to consequentialism, rule-based morality.

Exercises

Define in your own words the following terms:

1. consequentialism
2. ends/means distinction
3. situation ethics
4. hedonism
5. desire-satisfaction version of consequentialism
6. egoism
7. altruism
8. utilitarianism
9. rule-of-thumb approach to moral rules
10. special obligation

Review Questions

1. What determines the rightness and/or wrongness of an action for a consequentialist?
2. Why is consequentialism committed to rejecting the view that there are actions which are intrinsically right or wrong?
3. Why are all consequentialist theories a form of situation ethics?
4. What are the advantages and disadvantages of hedonism? Of desire-satisfaction consequentialism?
5. What are the advantages and disadvantages of egoism? Of altruism?
6. What are the main advantages of consequentialism?
7. How do consequentialists view traditional moral rules?
8. What are the main objections to consequentialism? What are the different strategies consequentialists adopt to meet them?

Questions for Further Thought

1. Many people are troubled by the consequentialist thesis that the ends justify the means. Other people have no difficulty with this thesis; they argue that the ends are all we have for justifying the means. Critically evaluate this debate.
2. How would a hedonist respond to the objections raised by the case of the death-bed promise and that of the sadist and masochist?
3. Suppose you are an altruist. What arguments would you use to decide whether to include the consequences for fetuses? For future generations? For animals?

4. The problem raised for altruism, that of how to compare the gains for some and the losses for others, is often called the problem of the interpersonal comparison of utility. Explain why it is such a difficult question. Do you see any solution to it?

5. Consider the following objection, often called a *slippery slope objection,* to making the exception and to torturing the terrorist: "Once you make a single exception to the rule, once you torture even one person, you make it harder to avoid such actions in the future. It is hard to stop once you start. Therefore, in the long run, the consequences are best if we make no exceptions to such moral rules." Do you think that consequentialists should accept this argument in the case of the rule against torture? In connection with other rules?

6. Suppose that consequentialists were to claim that the reason why we should put the interests of people who are special to us before the interests of strangers is that doing so will produce the best consequences because it promotes the development of special relations which are a source of much desire-satisfaction. Would this be a satisfactory response? Could a similar consequentialist response be offered for respecting rights and seeking justice?

Chapter Two

Rule-Based Morality

2·1 INTRODUCTION TO MORAL RULES

We saw in the last chapter that one of the implications of consequentialism is that traditional moral systems have overemphasized adherence to rules. The consequentialist believes that moral rules are useful only as rules of thumb, telling us which sorts of actions will *normally* lead to the best consequences.

In this chapter, we will consider a second approach to morality, one that differs with consequentialism on precisely this point. *Rule-based morality* (also called the *deontological approach*) proposes that an action is right if it conforms with a proper moral rule (where that rule does not necessarily refer to the consequences of the action), and that an action is wrong when it violates such a rule. On this second approach, moral rules are essential to morality, not merely useful rules of thumb.

As you might expect, there are a great many versions of rule-based morality, each differing from the others according to the rules it advocates, the importance it ascribes to different rules, its flexibility in making exceptions, and so forth. In this section, we will consider the types of rules that are most widely adopted by these moral systems.

Among the most commonly accepted types of rules are those which ascribe intrinsic value (usually negative) to an action. Examples of such rules are prohibitions against killing, against lying, and against violating the privacy of others. What these rules say is that the very character of certain actions makes them impermissible.

It is important to note the relation between this type of rule and the belief in certain fundamental human rights. It is widely agreed that people have a right to life and that there is a corresponding duty on other people not to violate that right by killing someone. Thus, the moral rule which prohibits killing protects the right to life. Similarly, it is widely agreed that people have a right to privacy, and that other people have a duty not to interfere with that privacy. Thus, the moral rule against violating the privacy of others protects the right to privacy.

According to the deontological approach to morality, when the rule in question prohibits certain types of actions, the prohibition holds even if performing the action would result in beneficial consequences in a particular case. The idea is that performing these actions is an illegitimate means that cannot be justified even if the ends are good ones. Some proponents of these rules treat the prohibitions in question as absolute. Others may be willing to allow for exceptions in the most extreme examples. However, all proponents of these rules maintain that, at least in most cases, the means cannot justify the ends. This stands in clear contrast to consequentialism, which says that the ends can justify *any* means, providing that the value of the ends is sufficiently great to outweigh the evil of the means.

One final point about this type of rule. Whether the rule is treated as absolute or allowed to have exceptions in certain extreme cases, the proponents of the rule think that, except perhaps in a few very special cases, the performance of that type of action is always wrong. Consequently, the proponents of this rule-based morality place far less emphasis on the examination of particular circumstances and particular situations. In this respect, as well as in the many already indicated, they are in strong disagreement with consequentialists, who advocate a form of situation-ethics.

The second widely accepted type of moral rules are those that make reference both to the character of the action performed and to the relation between the actor and the parties affected. Examples include the rules to honor one's parents, to aid one's friends in time of distress, to nurture one's children, to keep one's promises, and so on. In each of these cases, the rule requires a certain type of action toward people to whom one has a special relation. Notice that the same type of action is not required toward other people.

We saw in the previous chapter that one of the implications of consequentialism is that morality does not consider the special relationships in which we stand to other people. It is just these sorts of relationships that we are now talking about, and the rules concerning them (which are commonly found in rule-based moral systems) help differentiate deontological from consequentialist moral systems.

A third category of commonly accepted moral rules includes those which call upon us to reward or punish people in proportion to their deserts. Among the rules of this sort is the requirement that we punish criminals in proportion to the seriousness of their crime and reward achievers in accordance with the merit of their accomplishment. As we saw in the last chapter, these are the rules that are so central to our notion of justice.

Naturally, there are serious disagreements as to who deserves more and who less punishment, and who deserves more and who fewer rewards. Such disagreements reflect different conceptions of merit and demerit. For instance, some people say that students should be rewarded in proportion to the quality of the work they produce. Others feel that a more just method is to reward students in proportion to the effort they expend in producing the work. We are not concerned here with trying to settle this dispute; all we want to do is point out that proponents of each reward system are proposing moral rules of justice of the type with which we are concerned.

The final type of widely held rule is the general moral rule to do those actions which produce the best consequences. For the adherents of rule-based moral systems that contain such a general rule, the difference between rule-based morality and consequentialism is that the former contains many other rules as well, rules which very often take precedence over this general rule.

While this brief survey is by no means complete, it is sufficient to point out one of the obvious strengths of the deontological, or rule-based, approach to morality. As we saw in the previous chapter, there are many who feel that consequentialism is an inadequate moral theory because it fails to take into account anything other than the consequences of an action. Rule-based moralities, on the contrary, do just this. While they differ on the particular rules they advocate, they all are capable of dealing with the many aspects of morality which consequentialism neglects.

In a later section of this chapter we will look at both the strengths and weaknesses of rule-based moralities. But before doing so, we need to consider two fundamental questions about rule-based moralities: Which rules are the proper moral rules? and How do we know which rules they are? Since there are so many different rule-based moralities, and since they contain different moral rules, any believer in a particular rule-based morality must confront these questions. We will look at possible answers in the next section.

2•2 THE SOURCE OF MORAL RULES

There are four major types of answers to the two questions just raised: the theological answer, the societal answer, the consequentialist answer, and the intuitionist answer. We will examine each of them in turn.

The *theological* answer claims that the proper moral rules are those which God wills us to follow. Proponents of this answer usually go on to claim that we know which rules they are because God has revealed them to us as those which he expects us to live by. The problem with this answer is that it is indefensible. Different religions put forward differing claims about the will of God, and each purports to be backed up by divine revelation. So an appeal to the will of God and to divine revelation to resolve the problem of conflicting moral rules won't help us. There is just as much conflict about what is God's will and about what God has revealed to us as there is about what the proper moral rules are.

Let us put this point another way. Suppose you were the lifeboat captain of the *William Brown* and that you believed you ought to follow the proper moral rules relevant to this case, not just calculate the consequences of your actions. Obviously, you would still have a problem, because there are many different moral rules which people have advocated and which have differing implications for this case. For example, there is the rule that one ought never to kill an innocent human being. If you believe that this moral rule is proper, then it would be wrong to decide to force anyone overboard. On the other hand, there is the rule that one should always try to save as many lives as possible. If you believe that this moral rule is proper, then you should decide in favor of forcing some people overboard in order to save the lives of everyone else. But which of these moral rules is the proper rule? Well, the theological answer says that it is the rule which God wants us to follow and which He has revealed to us as His will. But which rule is that? Surely, there is as much conflict about that theological question as there is about the original moral question. It may well be true that the correct moral rule is the one which God wants us to follow, but the theological approach to rule-based morality does not help us decide what to do. Unless we have clear evidence about the will of God, we must turn to other sources to provide us with good information about what the proper moral rules are.

The *societal* approach adopts a very different view of this matter. According to it, the proper moral rules are the ones believed in by most members of the society in which the agent finds himself. It is this social consensus about morality that determines what is right and wrong. Thus, as long as that society believes in a particular set of moral rules, then actions performed by members of the society in conformance with these rules are always morally right. By this standard, then, the guards at Hitler's concentration camps or at Stalin's work camps acted in a morally correct fashion because they followed the moral rules believed in by the majority of the members of their society.

If we want to reject this consequence and say that some actions are wrong even if they are in conformity with the views of most members of the given society, then we must reject the societal answer. Furthermore, this approach is highly problematic in all the difficult moral cases that one normally encounters. Consider once more our lifeboat example and the conflicting moral rules that might be put forward. Is it clear that one rule is favored by most members of the captain's society? Isn't it more likely that no rule is favored over another? Aren't most people in doubt about such cases? If, indeed, there is no consensus among the society, then according to the societal approach, there is no such thing as the proper moral rule, and therefore there is no difference between right and wrong in this case. If we want to reject these implications, we must reject the societal approach.

There is an important difference between our criticism of the theological approach and our criticism of the societal approach. We have tried to show that the societal approach—which claims that the right action is the one that conforms with the moral rule accepted by most members of the agent's society—offers an inappropriate definition of the "right" action. Conversely, when we criticized the theological approach—which claims that the right action is the action in conformity with the moral rule that God wishes us to follow—we were not discrediting the definition itself; rather, we were claiming that this approach simply does not help us resolve the difficult moral problems we must confront.

These problems, and others of a similar nature, have led most moral theorists to conclude that rule-based moralities must be based upon something other than the will of God or the judgment of a society. Therefore, the two approaches most commonly adopted today appeal either to the consequences of adopting a particular set of moral rules or to our supposed faculty of moral intuition.

The *consequentialist* answer claims that the proper moral rules are those which, when followed, lead to better consequences than one would get from following any alternative moral rule. This answer, which we will refer to as *rule consequentialism* to distinguish it from the *act consequentialism* of the previous chapter, says that, in effect, the rightness of a particular action lies in its conformity with the proper moral rule; the properness of the moral rule, in turn, is based on the value of the consequences of it being followed. An example will help clarify this.

Consider the moral rule prohibiting the killing of innocent human beings. Rule consequentialists, like most believers in rule-based moralities, claim that this is a proper moral rule. When asked to justify this claim, they say it is a proper moral rule because following it will, in the long run, lead to better consequences than will not following it. Once the rule has been established as proper, it ought to be followed in all cases in which it applies. Thus, refraining from killing an innocent human being in each applicable case is the right thing to do because it conforms with a proper moral rule.

At first glance, there might seem to be little difference between rule consequentialism and the more standard act consequentialism which we analyzed in Chapter 1. A closer examination, however, suggests why people believe that there is a significant difference between these two approaches. Once more, our lifeboat example can be used to help bring out the difference. Suppose, for the sake of discussion, that in this case the best consequences are those that will follow from throwing some people overboard. If this is true, then the act consequentialist is committed to the belief that the right thing to do is to throw some people overboard. For the act consequentialist says that even if we normally produce the best consequences by not killing innocent human beings (that is, that the rule against killing innocent human beings is a good rule of thumb), we should, nevertheless, make an exception in those rare and tragic cases in which doing so will lead to the best consequences. The rule consequentialist, in contrast, sees things differently. He says that if following the rule against killing innocent human beings will in general lead to the best results, then that rule is a proper moral rule and should be followed in every case in which it applies. Thus, even in our lifeboat case (that is, even upon the supposition that the best consequences will come about by pushing the people overboard), the rule against killing should still be followed.

Notice that rule consequentialism is an attempt to obtain the benefits of both consequentialism and rule-based morality. Rule consequentialism, like traditional act consequentialism, sees the moral life as leading to the best consequences, taking into account all those affected. At the same time, it ascribes greater significance to moral rules than to mere rules of thumb. Rule consequentialism appears to be quite attractive, but it presents several major difficulties. Let's look at each of them separately.

To begin with, it is very hard to see why we should follow the rules in all cases. Since the rule consequentialist, like the act consequentialist, agrees that the moral life has value because it leads to the best consequences, taking into account the interest of all those affected, then why shouldn't we break the rule in question in those special cases in which doing so would lead to better consequences? If the whole justification of the rule is that following it will lead to the best consequences, then isn't it nonsensical to follow it in cases in which it will not lead to the best consequences? In short, rule consequentialists find it very difficult to explain the emphasis that their approach places on rules when the rules are treated as something more than just rules of thumb.

Second, it is not clear that there really is a difference between act consequentialism and rule consequentialism. In terms of our lifeboat case and the supposition that the best consequences will come about by throwing some people overboard, the rule consequentialist suggests that he is free to object to pushing people overboard whereas the act consequentialist is required to approve that act. Is this difference real? To decide, let's consider the following two rules:

Rule 1: Never kill any innocent human beings.
Rule 2: Never kill any innocent human beings except when they will die anyway in the very near future and when killing them is necessary to save the lives of many other innocent human beings.

Rule 2 accepts the prohibition of Rule 1 except for special circumstances. It seems likely that following Rule 2 will have better consequences than following Rule 1. Careful reflection reveals, then, that there is no real difference between the conclusion of the act consequentialist and that of the rule consequentialist in this particular case. And, more generally, given that we can always make our rules more specific and build into them exceptions involving favorable consequences, it seems likely that there can be no differences between act consequentialism and rule consequentialism. Therefore, those who seek a rule-based morality as an alternative to act consequentialism would do best to ground the properness of moral rules in something other than the beneficial consequences of following them. For these people, perhaps the answer lies in the faculty of moral intuition.

The *intuitionist* answer claims that the proper moral rules are those which possess the intrinsic characteristics of being proper, and that the right actions (taken in accord with these rules) are those which possess the intrinsic characteristics of rightness. We know which actions and rules have these intrinsic characteristics through our special faculty of moral intuition. Let's look at this explanation more closely.

The first three answers that we considered — the theological, the societal, and the consequentialist — all agree in stating that the properness of a moral rule is not an intrinsic characteristic of that rule. According to the first two answers, properness is attributed to a moral rule either by God or by society. And according to the third answer, properness depends on the consequences of following the rule. But the intuitionist answer claims that the properness of a moral rule is an intrinsic feature of that rule and that the rightness of a particular action (taken in accord with that rule) is an intrinsic feature of that action. In short, the intuitionist asserts that morality is an intrinsic feature of the world.

Since it is impossible to perceive with our senses the rightness of an action and/or the properness of a rule, how are we to know whether these characteristics are possessed by specific actions or rules? The intuitionist says that, much as we have senses through which we learn about the observable features of the world, so we have a special intellectual capacity that enables us to intuitively know the properness of rules and the rightness of actions.

Many intuitionist writers go on to claim that moral intuitions are absolutely certain — that is, they are never wrong — and so we have no reason to ever revise them. For the purposes of this book, however, the intuitionist argument does not extend to such an extreme; rather, it simply says that we have a capacity for moral intuition which gives us reasonable beliefs about the properness of rules and the rightness of actions, and that these beliefs — like any reasonable beliefs about the world — are subject to later revision.

Many intuitionists are divided in their interpretation of this approach, with some claiming that our moral intuitive faculty can perceive only the properness of specific moral *rules* and others claiming that our intuitions can only be about the rightness and wrongness of specific *actions*. Our version of intuitionism agrees with neither of these approaches. It is willing to admit both types of intuitions, and it claims, moreover, that each type can be used in the process of refining and revising the other. To illustrate, we refer back to our lifeboat example.

Many intuitionists would analyze the case as follows: On the one hand, we have a clear intuition that it is wrong to take the life of an innocent human being. On the other hand, this is an instance in which if we do nothing everyone will shortly die anyway, but if we take some lives we can save the rest. Our intuition in this case is that it is right to take some innocent lives in order to save the others. We have, therefore, a conflict between our general intuition and our intuitions about specific cases. To resolve this conflict, we modify our general rule so as to claim that it is wrong to take the lives of innocent human beings except in certain extreme situations, such as this one.

The intuitionist position, while highly controversial, seems to be the best foundation open to us for a rule-based morality. In the rest of the book, we will be contrasting utilitarianism, as our preferred version of consequentialism, with an intuition-based version of deontological morality containing the type of rules discussed above. First, though, we will spend the remainder of this chapter assessing some of the general strengths and weaknesses of rule-based morality.

2·3 STRENGTHS AND WEAKNESSES OF RULE-BASED MORALITIES

Interestingly, the strengths and weaknesses of rule-based moralities are closely related to the strengths and weaknesses of consequentialism. That is, many of the strengths of consequentialism are the weaknesses of rule-based moralities and rule-based moralities accommodate many of the problems of consequentialism. It would be nice if one could find a way to combine the two, but as yet no one has come up with a suitable compromise.

We have seen that the fundamental weakness of consequentialism is that it presents too monolithic a theory of morality. By claiming that the only factor relevant to evaluating the morality of an action is the action's consequences, the approach leaves out too many crucial aspects of ordinary moral consciousness, such as special obligations to people, a respect for individual rights, and a desire for justice. We have also seen that rule-based moralities can accommodate these aspects of ordinary moral consciousness by providing special rules to deal with these issues. This is one obvious strength of rule-based moralities.

Moreover, even among those who believe in making exceptions, there are many who see consequentialism as allowing for *too many* exceptions to traditional moral rules. These critics argue that as soon as the consequences of breaking a rule are even slightly better than the consequences of keeping it, the consequentialist tells us to break the rule. They see the consequentialist as too permissive in allowing for exceptions and maintain that it is appropriate to make exceptions in cases of great emergency, where that term is admittedly vague, but not in instances where doing so merely produces slightly better consequences. They would agree, for example, with the need to make an exception to the rule against torturing in the case (discussed in Chapter 1) of the terrorist who has planted a bomb that is about to go off and kill thousands of people. But they would object to torturing him if such punishment resulted only in, say, an admission of guilt and not in information about where to find the bomb. In short, many people feel that consequentialism, with its rule-of-thumb approach to morality, does not have enough respect for the significance of moral rules. For this reason, they prefer a rule-based morality, where the rules can be modified to accommodate our moral intuitions about needed exceptions.

Let's turn now to some of the weaknesses of rule-based moralities.

The Problem of Conflicting Moral Rules

In Chapter 1 we saw that among the most difficult types of moral problems are those where two moral rules, each plausible, come into conflict. As an example we used the case of a judge trying to decide whether to stop a newspaper from publishing information about an accused criminal, where that information might interfere with the accused's right to a fair trial. Consequentialism has a well-articulated approach for dealing with this type of problem: disregard both conflicting rules and do whatever will lead to the best consequences. Deontologists, or believers in rule-based moralities, do not have such a clear-cut approach to handling such conflicts. Instead, intuitionists, in particular, hope that via the process of attuning our intuitions about rules to our intuitions about particular cases so that they fit each other, we will develop a set of moral rules sophisticated enough to avoid this type of conflict. At the moment, however, this is still a hope, not a reality, and rule-based moralities, including the intuitionist approach, do not adequately deal with the problem of conflicting moral rules.

The Process of Moral Reasoning

There is something very tidy and straightforward about the consequentialist approach to moral reasoning. One lists the alternatives, determines their consequences, and weighs the value of each. While carrying out these steps may not be as tidy and straightforward as the theory sets them down, the consequentialist at least knows what he is supposed to do. The deontologist, on the other hand, is rather at a loss in this respect. Even the most helpful of the rule-based moralities, the intuitionist approach, relies on imprecise admonitions to adjust one's intuitions about general rules to those about particular cases. Moreover, there is the ever-present possibility of people having conflicting intuitions and of our not being able to come to some agreement based on our intuitions about what are the proper rules. The consequentialist says we would do best to focus instead on his method of reasoning.

Intuitionists, naturally, reject this conclusion. They not only feel that their method has the potential for eventually attaining a clear-cut conclusion but that the consequentialist underemphasizes the difficulty of implementing his approach. They question whether one can really ascertain the consequences of all possible actions or be able to judge their value.

As you proceed through this text, you will have many chances to see for yourself, in the context of real moral issues, whether the process of moral reasoning is more difficult in the intuitionist, deontological approach to morality or in the consequentialist approach. And by the end of the book, you will be in a good position to judge the extent to which each approach provides a usable procedure for moral reasoning.

The Goal of Morality

We pointed out in the last chapter that one of the strengths of consequentialism is that it offers an explanation of why we take morality so seriously: by doing the right thing we will bring about the best consequences for those affected. Deontologists do not have such a clear-cut reason for why morality is so important. They are forced to fall back on the argument that morality is important per se, and that is just a fundamental truth about the universe. The consequentialists see this inability as an important drawback of rule-based moralities.

In this chapter and the last one, we have developed the major ideas about the two basic approaches to morality. We have examined several types of each, and have chosen utilitarianism as our version of consequentialism and the intuitionist approach as our version of deontological morality. We will contrast these approaches throughout the book, exposing their strengths and weaknesses as we examine not only the theories which support them but also the practical implications they hold for a wide variety of contemporary moral problems.

Exercises

Define in your own words the following terms:

1. deontological approach
2. theological approach to moral rules
3. societal approach to moral rules

4. rule consequentialism vs. act consequentialism
5. moral intuitionism
6. conflicting moral rules

Review Questions

1. What determines the rightness and/or wrongness of an action for a deontologist?
2. What are the main types of rules normally introduced into deontological moral systems?
3. What are the major suggested sources of moral rules?
4. What are the strengths and weaknesses of the theological source of moral rules? Of the societal source? Of the consequentialist source? Of the intuitionist source?
5. How does rule consequentialism attempt to capture the strengths of both act consequentialism and deontological morality?
6. What types of moral intuitions do we have according to the version of intuitionism presented in this chapter? How do we use these different types of intuitions?
7. What are the main strengths of deontological moral systems? How do they relate to the weaknesses of consequentialism?
8. What are the main weaknesses of deontological moral systems? How do they relate to the strengths of consequentialism?

Questions for Further Thought

1. Critically evaluate the dispute between those who would treat moral rules as absolute and those who would make exceptions in extreme cases. If you decide in favor of making these exceptions, explain how you would decide when a case is extreme enough to justify an exception.
2. The chapter lists certain main types of rules which a deontological system normally contains. Are there others? In particular, do we need special rules about such virtues as courage and temperance?
3. How might defenders of the theological and/or societal approach respond to the objections raised in the chapter?
4. Consider the following defense by a rule consequentialist of following the rules in all cases: "Morality requires us to treat like cases alike. If we make exceptions in a few cases, we are being unfair, because like cases are being treated differently. That is why we must treat moral rules as more than rules of thumb." Is this an adequate response to the claim that rule consequentialism is an absurd form of rule worship?
5. Do you think our intuitions are a source of insight into objective value features of the world or are they just disguised versions of

our personal and social prejudices? Is it relevant, in answering this question, to find out whether people with different backgrounds have different intuitions?

6. Some people feel that deontological moral systems, with their many and varied types of rules, are impossible to adopt because we have no way of reconciling the demands of these different rules. Others claim that this complexity simply reflects the complexity of the moral facts of the world. Critically evaluate this debate.

Chapter Three

Value Problems in the Criminal Justice System

T he first set of moral issues we will consider relate to the goals and functions of the criminal justice system in America. Since this system can limit the ways in which people act by punishing those who break the rules society creates, it is not surprising that issues surrounding the criminal justice system give rise to many moral problems. In particular, we will be concerned with such basic questions as why society limits behavior in this way, what goals society hopes to achieve by punishing people when they break the rules, and what means of punishment the system should employ.

While our focus is on the foundations of the criminal justice system and the basic values it embodies, much of what we say will have substantial implications for the practical problems of law and order that are frequently in the news. Also, in looking at the basic structure of the criminal justice system in America today, we will pay some attention to alternatives to that system. Finally, and most importantly, we will examine the basic theoretical moral questions raised by each aspect of the system, thereby setting the stage for the two chapters that follow. In Chapter 4 we will look at the utilitarian's answers to these questions, and in Chapter 5 we will see how the deontologist answers them.

3·1 CRIMINAL JUSTICE AS A SYSTEM

Philosophers often speak about the need to develop a theory of punishment, but it is important to keep in mind that in the criminal justice system, punishment is the last stage in a very complex process. What we need to develop, then, is a theory that can settle the many questions that arise in connection with each element in the system. In this section we outline the main features of the criminal justice system, and in the following sections we explore the main theoretical and moral issues that pertain to the system.

It is useful to think of the criminal justice system as having four major elements: the process of prohibiting actions and assigning penalties, the agent who violates those prohibitions, the mechanism for investigating a violation and determining the perpetrator, and the punishment meted out to the violator. We will look at each of these components in turn.

The Process of Prohibiting Actions and Assigning Penalties. The United States has many criminal justice systems. For instance, there is a federal system, and there are separate systems for each state. Every criminal justice system must have some process by which various actions are prohibited and penalties for violating those prohibitions are assigned.

Typically, some of the actions that state systems prohibit and treat as criminal are those which were prohibited under the old Common Law of England. But many of the crimes recognized by state systems are the result of legislative procedures, and you should note that this component of the criminal justice system is essentially a legislative component. What the legislature does is prohibit a certain type of action and assign a penalty, or a range of penalties, for violations. Thus, the definition of a crime and the penalty attached to it cannot and does not deal with any specific case. But specific criminal acts are committed by specific individuals in specific circumstances, and, as we will see later in the chapter, some of the value problems associated with the criminal justice system are rooted in the difference between a general legislative act and a specific criminal act.

The Agent Who Violates Those Prohibitions.   The second major component of the criminal justice system is the criminal. Of course, there are many sorts of criminals, but, as we will see, the law most comfortably deals with an adult who, in a rational state of mind, calculates and freely chooses, for motives of personal gain, to violate a rule of society. Unfortunately, not all criminals fit this comfortable model. In fact, many major crimes are committed by juveniles, and juvenile criminals present a real problem for the criminal justice system. Other big problems concern how to handle people whose crimes were committed in a moment of passion or while under the influence of alcohol—those whose illegal acts were neither calculated nor committed rationally. These are only a few examples of the many types of criminals who do not fit the comfortable model and who thus force us to confront the question of whether all criminals can be dealt with by the same systems of criminal justice.

The Mechanism for Investigating a Violation and Determining the Perpetrator.   This component of the criminal justice system consists of the roles played by the police, the local prosecuting attorneys, and the judges and juries. The police investigate the violation and apprehend possible suspects, the local prosecuting attorney decides whether the evidence is sufficient to try the suspect, and the judge and jury decide whether the accused is indeed guilty.

It is this aspect of the criminal justice system which, in recent years, has come under the closest scrutiny and harshest criticism. There are several reasons for this. To begin with, many crimes are not seriously investigated, and among those that are, in many cases a suspect is not even apprehended. Furthermore, only some of the apprehended suspects are charged with a crime, and only some of those are eventually found guilty and sentenced. In short, of all the crimes committed, only a modest percentage are settled in that the perpetrator is convicted and punished. Many critics claim that the failings in this segment of the criminal justice system are primarily responsible for the decline in law and order in our society. Secondly, very few of those convicted are actually tried and convicted for the crime they perpetrated. A very large percentage of crimes for which a suspect is apprehended are settled by the process known as *plea bargaining*. Through that process, the criminal pleads guilty, thereby saving the state from having to try him, in return for the charge being lowered to a lesser crime than the one he has committed and in return for his receiving a lesser penalty. Many critics feel that this is another factor responsible for the decline of law and order in society.

The Punishment Meted Out to the Violator. In contemporary society there are four major types of penalties: fines, probation, imprisonment, and death. In recent years, the death penalty has been only rarely applied and there is continual litigation over its constitutionality.

One of the distinctive features of modern criminal justice systems is the heavy emphasis placed on probation and/or imprisonment. In earlier times, the penalties most often imposed were heavy fines and corporeal punishment. This trend has brought forth the observation by many critics that our prison and probation systems are inadequate for performing their functions. We would do well to remember that prisons are not an inevitable feature of a criminal justice system.

While the legislature is the typical agent responsible for assigning penalties to a certain type of crime, the judge is the typical agent responsible for sentencing the specific criminal. In some cases, the legislature gives the judge considerable leeway in deciding how to punish a specific criminal; in other cases, the legislature may mandate a specific penalty, allowing the judge no leeway whatsoever. It is often claimed that the former approach gives rise to unfairness, because different judges employ different standards in sentencing specific criminals. By the same token, others claim that the latter approach is unfair, because it fails to allow for the flexibility needed to deal with specific cases and specific circumstances.

With this brief survey of the major elements of our current system of criminal justice, we are now ready to look at each one in some depth, examining the value problems it poses for us.

3·2 THE DEFINITION OF A CRIME

When the state prohibits a certain action and threatens violators with a punishment, it, in effect, is attempting to coerce people into behaving in certain ways. Therefore, any analysis of a criminal justice system must begin by confronting certain fundamental value questions: What actions ought to be prohibited by law? and Why is it permissible to use the state's coercive mechanisms to prevent people from doing those actions?

The popular, standard answer to these questions, known as the *harm principle*, says that the state should prohibit actions when and only when their performance would lead to a harm to people who have not performed the action or who have not consented to the performance of the action. Thus, for example, it is permissible for the state to prohibit murder, and to threaten those who commit murder with serious penalties, because the act of murder would cause harm to someone who has not consented to the harm. The state therefore has the right to try to stop the murderer by threatening him with punishment.

By this reasoning, it would be wrong for the state to prohibit someone from holding certain religious beliefs, as various states have done in the past, since merely holding these beliefs can do no harm to anyone else. So, individuals have the right to hold these beliefs, and no state may prohibit such activity. The harm principle seems to make very good sense, and it is widely accepted. Nevertheless, there are a number of ways in which it can be criticized.

Victimless Crimes.   The criminal law in all jurisdictions of the United States prohibits many actions which at worst only harm the person who does them or those who have consented to having them done. Suicide and prostitution are two prime examples. Drug use, usury, and driving a motorcycle without a helmet are others. In all, there are a great many prohibitions against many different types of *victimless crimes*, or crimes that, at most, harm only those who commit them or those adults who have voluntarily consented to them.

Many people would do away with a large number of these victimless crimes. They contend that the criminal justice system should legalize the use of marijuana, prostitution involving consenting adults, suicide, and other such activities. Only a few people, however, advocate that we do away with all victimless crimes. Most people, for example, support the idea that usury should be a crime, and many are in favor of keeping the motorcycle helmet act. So unless we mean to do away with all victimless crimes, we must reject the harm principle and find some more satisfactory theory as to which actions should be prohibited by law.

Conspiracies and Attempts.   In most jurisdictions, people can be punished for *attempting* to commit certain crimes or for *conspiring* with others to commit those crimes. Thus, attempted murder is a crime, even if the attempt fails miserably and no one is harmed.

Similarly, conspiring to kidnap someone is a crime, even if the conspiracy is never carried out and no one is harmed. The law has a difficult problem trying to distinguish between mere speculation about committing a crime (which is not punishable) and actual attempts and conspiracies (which are punishable). Nevertheless, there are many clear-cut cases of true attempts and conspiracies which are normally punished even though no one is harmed. In fact, some people believe that attempted murder, for example, should carry the same penalty as actual murder. After all, they argue, in both cases the criminal is trying to do the same thing; why should one be punished less just because he failed? Leaving aside that question, the existence of criminal penalties for attempted crimes and for conspiracies suggest that we need a more satisfactory theory about which actions should be punishable by law.

Legitimate Harms. Suppose you own a grocery store and I open a store across the street, and compete with you very effectively. My action will certainly harm you. Moreover, it is unlikely that you will have consented to my harmful action. Nevertheless, it would seem implausible to make my action a crime, unless I compete in a fashion that seems grossly unfair or inappropriate. Historically, there have been societies that have prohibited someone from competing with an established business. But under our free-enterprise system, competition is viewed as healthy and beneficial to society. How, then, are we to reconcile these two views? If we say that opening a competitive business which results in harm to one's neighbor is not a criminal act, then we must reject the harm principle, which says that people should be punished if and only if their actions harm other people who have not consented to being harmed.

Obviously, we need to find a more satisfactory principle as to which actions ought to be treated as criminal. Such a principle will need to cover the many counter examples we found to the harm principle and it will also need to provide us with a satisfactory explanation as to *why* the state may legitimately coerce people in the cases which it allows as legitimate. In the next two chapters we will see how the utilitarian and the deontologist, respectively, deal with these questions.

3·3 THE CRIMINAL

Historically, we can find examples of societies in which everyone who commits a criminal act is punished, and all those who commit the same act are punished to the same extent. More typically, however, societies recognize a variety of excuses, mitigations, and justifications for committing a crime.

An *excuse* is an argument to the effect that while the crime was indeed committed and wrong done, the criminal should not be punished in any way, because he was not responsible for what he did. One well-known excuse that the law recognizes is that of insanity. Thus, if an insane person shoots and kills someone, our law says that even though what he did was wrong, he should not be punished because he is not responsible for his actions. (No doubt, he will be confined to a mental institution.)

A *mitigation* is an argument to the effect that while the person did commit the crime, he should not be punished to the usual extent, either because the crime is not considered as bad as it normally would be or because the criminal is not fully responsible for his actions. Say, for example, that a man shoots his best friend upon discovering him in bed with his wife. Our criminal justice system punishes the husband less severely than it does most murderers, in part because the murderer acted in a fit of rage and was therefore less responsible than normal, and in part because the circumstances that provoked his behavior makes the act, while still wrong, not as bad as it normally would be.

A *justification* is an argument to the effect that while the person did commit the crime, there was nothing wrong with committing it in that particular case. A good example is self-defense, which claims that the crime had to be committed in order to protect oneself from harm.

The point is that society recognizes a wide variety of excuses, mitigations, and justifications surrounding the commitment of a crime and that punishment cannot be administered solely on the grounds that a law was violated. Something more must be present. The standard legal formula is that punishment is called for only when a guilty mind accompanies the guilty act. But this formula is not very helpful in deciding who should be punished and who should not, because it does not tell us what constitutes a guilty mind. It is helpful, however, in reminding us that the act of punishment presupposes a certain conception of the criminal and his mind.

As we stated in section 3.1, we are most comfortable with punishing a sane adult who after rational calculation freely chooses, for motives of personal gain, to violate the criminal law in a way that harms others by violating their rights. In such cases, there seems to be little basis for excuses, mitigations, and justifications. But we have seen that there are many cases that do not fit this model. And we are often in the uncomfortable position of having to decide whether someone should be punished. To help with this decision, we need a theory that will tell us what the criminal must be like before he should be punished.

Such a theory must do two things. To begin with, it must deal with all the nonstandard cases, giving us ways to distinguish the legitimate from the illegitimate excuses, mitigations, and justifications. Second, it must help us deal with certain fundamental challenges to the whole system of criminal law, such as the argument that lawbreakers should be treated like patients and helped rather than punished. According to this view, committing a crime is like getting sick. Psychological forces over which the person has no control are responsible for the crime, and the criminal should simply be treated for his sickness. Others argue that crime is primarily a product of desperation and poverty. On this view, crime calls neither for punishment nor for treatment but for poverty programs and eradication of the conditions that lead to crime. Both these challenges to our present system claim that a proper understanding of the criminal must necessarily lead to the abolishment of punishment. Any adequate theory of the criminal, then, must provide us with appropriate responses to this claim.

In the next two chapters we will examine the theories that utilitarians and deontologists have built to incorporate their views about the criminal. Each theory provides an alternative approach to excuses, mitigations, and justifications, and each also provides an alternative way to deal with these fundamental objections.

3·4 APPREHENSION AND CONVICTION

A fundamental problem in the area of investigation, apprehension, and conviction of criminals stems from the fact that the criminal justice system has conflicting goals. One important goal is to catch and convict criminals. This tells us that the system should be structured so as to maximize the number of people who are apprehended for and convicted of criminal actions. Another major goal of the system is to protect the innocent. This goal suggests that the system should be structured so as to minimize the number of innocent parties who are unduly interfered with, apprehended, and convicted.

Before we can begin to see how these two conflicting goals might be reconciled, it is important to understand how they come into conflict. At the heart of the conflict is the issue of what degree of evidence to require before someone can be convicted. The more evidence we require, the fewer criminals we will catch and convict — the guilty will escape for want of sufficient evidence to prove their guilt. If the requirement for evidence is low, fewer guilty parties will escape, but we will have more cases involving innocent parties mistakenly apprehended and convicted on the basis of the modest evidence required. In sum, the question of what amount of evidence to require before somebody can be convicted is more than a technical issue of law. It is a question whose resolution depends on how we confront some of our fundamental social values.

It is often said that American law places far greater emphasis on protecting the innocent from being falsely accused than on ensuring that the guilty will be convicted. Because our legal system imposes a requirement that criminal conviction be based on evidence that establishes guilt beyond any reasonable doubt, it is seen as committed to the belief that it is better that a thousand guilty parties escape than that one innocent party be convicted and punished.

For the sake of perspective, you should keep in mind that the phrase "beyond any reasonable doubt" is of little practical guidance to juries and has minimal theoretical content. What, exactly, is the level of evidence required for conviction by our justice system? Do we really believe that it is better that a thousand guilty parties escape conviction than that one innocent party be convicted? And regardless of what we believe, what should we think about these questions? These are important issues, and in the next two chapters we will see what the utilitarians and the intuitionists have to say about them.

Another important set of value questions concerning our system of apprehension and conviction raise strong moral questions about ways of obtaining evidence. We would not, for example, be happy with a system that routinely obtains evidence through the use of torture. In part, we would not trust such a system, because under torture most people will confess to anything. But our primary unhappiness with such a system would stem from our belief that certain means for obtaining information are morally wrong and should not be employed. There are certain requirements and constraints regarding methods of obtaining evidence embodied in our constitutional provisions. The prohibition against illegal searches and seizures, the right to refuse to testify when on trial, and the right to demand due process of law are some examples. In recent years, these requirements have been extensively elaborated. Suspects must be warned of their rights, entitled to counsel at a wide variety of stages, and so forth.

Clearly, we want our criminal justice system to apprehend and convict those who are guilty. At the same time, we want the system to employ in this process only legitimate means; that is, we want to guarantee to everyone due processes of law. Once more, there is a trade-off inherent in satisfying these two goals. The fewer constraints we put on the system of apprehension and conviction the better our chances of apprehending and convicting the guilty. The price for doing this, however, is to disregard some of the rights of suspects. The more we pay attention to these rights—by imposing greater constraints on the process of apprehension and conviction—the fewer guilty parties we will be able to apprehend and convict. Currently, these issues are the subjects of much debate, as people question whether we have made the proper choice in this trade-off.

Some people claim that Supreme Court decisions made during the last 20 years have overly emphasized protection of suspects' rights. Others argue that many investigative procedures are still in violation of suspects' rights and that we have not done enough to ensure protection of these rights and to guarantee due process of law. In the next two chapters we will analyze the implications of the utilitarian and deontological approaches to these issues.

One set of questions about this aspect of the justice system remains to be considered. As we pointed out in section 3.1, only a small proportion of people who commit crimes are actually tried and convicted. Further, of those who are convicted, most are convicted on the basis of a confession given as a result of plea bargaining. That is, in return for a promise of a lighter penalty, or of being charged with a lighter crime, the criminal pleads guilty without a trial and is sentenced by the judge in accordance with the promises made.

Is this a desirable feature of our system? It can be argued that plea bargaining helps ensure speedier convictions, keeps the courts from being overcrowded with cases, and sees to it that the guilty are at least punished to some degree. It can also be argued that plea bargaining is used manipulatively in cases where there is insufficient evidence to ensure conviction. Suspects, told they will fare worse if brought to trial, confess out of fear or ignorance to crimes they didn't commit. Opponents of plea bargaining object to the practice partly for this reason and partly because it involves practices that are questionable on moral grounds. We will look at these issues more fully in the next two chapters.

3·5 PUNISHMENT

There are a number of issues that concern this last stage of the criminal justice system—the punishment of criminals. These questions involve the types of punishment that are appropriate and the level of punishment that is appropriate. Let's look at each in turn.

As we noted earlier, the main punishments our system employs are fines, probation, and imprisonment. We are so used to this pattern of punishment that we often forget how new it is historically. The use of imprisonment as a major form of punishment emerged in Western societies as a great reform of the nineteen century. The early advocates of imprisonment viewed it as a humanitarian alternative to forced labor, corporeal punishment, and death. It was thought that in the context of this humane institution, rehabilitation would accompany punishment, and both the criminal and society would be better off.

These great hopes of the nineteenth century have been severely challenged by all studies of the realities of prison life. Rehabilitation programs have had little success, and for the most part, only lip service is now paid to that goal. Moreover, the brutal conditions inside the penitentiaries — in part the result of underfunding and in part the consequence of large numbers of criminals confined in one location — have reached such levels that the federal courts feel compelled to intervene to try to ensure at least a minimum standard of decency.

From the best intentions, this attempt at humane reform has turned into a mockery. How did this happen? The answer requires us to confront two fundamental questions: Is it possible to punish humanely, and Is imprisonment a plausible vehicle for obtaining our ends?

Another historical change that needs to be examined is the decline in the use of the death penalty. People have appealed to a number of different fundamental values in seeking to justify this phenomenon. Among the most widely cited is the view that it is wrong to deliberately take a human life, even when the intent is to punish the guilty. This view stands in stark contrast to the opposing view, which states that there are certain actions (most prominently, murder) which are so evil that anything less than the death penalty is unjust. It is this fundamental value disagreement that sparks the heated controversy over capital punishment.

A number of fundamental disputes also arise over the severity of punishment. To begin with, there is no systematic theory underlying our criminal laws that helps us decide which level of punishment to assign to specific types of crimes. Things have just grown up haphazardly. As a result, many people believe that we punish some crimes too harshly and other crimes too leniently, thereby creating injustices. It is often said, for example, that white-collar crimes, such as embezzlement or price fixing, are punished far too leniently as compared with street crimes, such as robbery or assault.

A second type of problem concerns the question of discretion for judges. Where the legislature has assigned a wide range of possible penalties for a given crime, leaving the actual penalty to be decided by the judge, certain gains and losses must be weighed. The main gain is that it allows the judge to fit the penalty to the particular circumstances of each case. This flexibility seems to permit a certain type of fairness. The main loss is that different judges will see things differently, and the result will be wide disparities in sentencing. This offends our sense of equity.

To conclude, we have found in the area of punishment as many value problems as we have found in all the other aspects of the criminal justice system. The message seems to be clear. We need a systematic moral approach that will help us find answers to these questions. Two such approaches, each in conflict with the other, will be examined, respectively, in the next two chapters.

Exercises

Define in your own words the following terms:

1. criminal justice system
2. plea bargaining
3. harm principle
4. victimless crime
5. excuse
6. mitigation
7. justification
8. due process of law
9. rehabilitation as a goal of punishment

Review Questions

1. What are the major elements of any criminal justice system? Where are these elements found in America's legal system?
2. What are the strengths and weaknesses of the harm principle?
3. What is a victimless crime? Why do victimless crimes pose a problem for those who believe in the harm principle?
4. Why do we often let people who have definitely committed a crime go unpunished? How does your answer relate to the requirement that a guilty act must be accompanied by a guilty mind?
5. What are the different goals of the system that apprehends and convicts criminals? How do these goals sometimes come into conflict?
6. What are the specific types of requirements summarized by the guarantee of due process of law?
7. What are the advantages and disadvantages of plea bargaining?
8. What are the advantages and disadvantages of imprisonment as a form of punishment?

Questions for Further Thought

1. Are there really any victimless crimes? Don't all these supposed victimless crimes involve indirect harm to other people?
2. What are the major excuses, mitigations, and justifications which you would want to introduce into a criminal justice system? How do these compare with the ones actually found in our system of criminal justice?

Chapter Four

The Criminal Justice System: A Utilitarian Approach

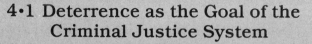

I n this chapter, we look at our moral questions relating to the criminal justice system from a utilitarian perspective. First, though, a word of caution: While all utilitarians agree on the basic theoretical framework that supports this approach, not all would offer the same analysis of the specific moral issues that will concern us here. This is not surprising. Different utilitarians working within the same framework could easily disagree over which proposals lead to the best consequences. Be aware, then, that this chapter presents *a* utilitarian approach to the criminal justice system, not *the only* utilitarian approach.

4·1 DETERRENCE AS THE GOAL OF THE CRIMINAL JUSTICE SYSTEM

Behind all utilitarian approaches to issues concerning the criminal justice system is the fundamental idea that this system is a necessary evil designed to deter people from engaging in criminal behavior. Two basic arguments support this view of punishment as an evil. First, a great many resources are required to construct such a system and carry out its operations. Society must make a huge investment in police, courts, and prisons. And the resources spent on these institutions are then unavailable to use in satisfying a wide variety of other preferences that people have. To the extent that these other preferences are not satisfied, the very existence of the criminal justice system and its operations represents an evil. Second, when someone is punished by the criminal justice system, that too creates an evil. After all, any punishment frustrates at least some of the criminal's preferences, for if that were not the case, the criminal would not be punished.

This last point deserves further explanation. There are some theories which maintain that since the criminal deserves to be punished, justice is done when such punishment is carried out, and because justice is intrinsically good, punishing criminals is intrinsically good. Utilitarianism rejects these conceptions on the grounds that the frustration of anyone's preferences is an evil. It makes no difference whose preferences they are, or even if they are criminal in nature.

Despite their view of punishment as an evil, utilitarians believe it is necessary. That is what they mean when they say that it is a necessary evil. They see it as necessary because they believe that the bad consequences it produces are outweighed by the good consequences which follow from its use.

What are these good consequences? The standard utilitarian claim is that they constitute the *deterrent effect* of the criminal justice system. By this utilitarians mean that the existence and use of the criminal justice system deters people from committing crimes. Those who are sufficiently afraid of being caught and punished will not commit crimes.

Utilitarians distinguish two types of deterrence — special deterrence and general deterrence. Special deterrence occurs when the criminal who is apprehended and punished does not commit a crime again either because (1) he is no longer capable of doing so on account of his punishment (e.g., he is in jail or dead) or (2) he is afraid to commit a crime again because he does not want to be punished any more. General deterrence occurs when the apprehension and punishment of some criminals results in *other* potential criminals not committing crimes they might otherwise have committed. An example of general deterrence is when you stop speeding when you see a policeman giving a speeder a ticket.

Because utilitarians believe that the existence and operation of the criminal justice system is a necessary evil, they also believe that its use should be confined only to those cases in which the evil really is outweighed by the deterrence achieved. Therefore, utilitarians argue, we should not punish criminals excessively in the sense of more than what is necessary to obtain the desired level of deterrence. In the nineteenth century, utilitarians were very active in promoting humane reforms in the criminal justice system. The main thrust of their argument was that society could satisfy its preference for deterrence with milder punishment techniques than those that were being employed; therefore, the excesses of the criminal justice system were unnecessary evils which should be abolished.

One final point. Some people challenge the assumption that the criminal justice system deters criminal behavior. They point out that all the crimes throughout human history have occurred despite the existence of this system. So how, they ask, can anyone believe that such a system deters criminal behavior? A moment's thought will show why this is not a good argument. For all we know, without the criminal justice system, many more crimes would have been committed. The fact that the criminal justice system has not deterred all crime does not mean that it has not deterred a great deal of crime. Despite its fallacy, this argument is useful because it points out the way in which the whole utilitarian approach to the criminal justice system depends on the empirical assumption that the existence of the system has a definite deterrent effect on crime.

4·2 A UTILITARIAN THEORY OF THE DEFINITION OF A CRIME

The first moral issue we took up in regard to the criminal justice system was the question of which actions the legislature should declare illegal. Recall that every time the legislature makes something a crime, it uses the criminal justice system as a coercive force to guide behavior. It is for this reason that we must understand not only *which* actions should be made crimes but *why* they should be made crimes.

From the utilitarian point of view, the decision to declare a certain type of action a crime has to be justified (like any other decision) in terms of the consequences of performing that action. Of course, there will be some bad consequences from making any type of action a crime. To begin with, many of those who desire to perform the action will see their desire frustrated because they fear being punished. Second, society will incur extra costs in providing the personnel and resources needed to deal with enforcing and punishing the new crime. As a result, those resources will not be available to use toward the satisfaction of other preferences. Finally, those who are caught committing the new crime will be punished, which, as we saw in section 4.1, also counts as a loss from the utilitarian point of view. On the other hand, there will be some good consequences from making the action a crime. Many people who otherwise would have performed that action will not do so out of fear of being punished. If the action in question could cause harm to someone, then the decision to make it a crime will spare some people from being hurt.

When all the good and bad consequences are listed and weighed against one another, the utilitarian can make a decision. If the losses are greater, the action should not be made a crime; if the gains are greater, it should be made a crime.

How does this utilitarian analysis compare with the harm principle? In many cases, the two will agree. Suppose we have a type of action that causes harm to others who have not consented to it. In this case, it is likely that the utilitarian will agree, for the most part, with the harm principle in saying that the action should be a crime. After all, it is probable that the gains brought about by making the action a crime (prevention of harm to those who would otherwise be harmed) will outweigh the losses incurred from making it a crime (extra administrative costs, frustrated desires of potential criminals). Thus, murder, for example, should be a crime because in most cases the gains from preventing murders outweigh the losses of the extra administrative burden on the criminal justice system and the frustrated desires of potential murderers.

Now suppose that we have a type of action that harms no one or that harms only those who commit the act or who consent to it being committed. In such cases it is also likely that the utilitarian will agree, for the most part, with the harm principle in saying that the action should not be made a crime. Here, since no one can be harmed by the action, there can be no benefits from preventing it. But even if the perpetrators or those who consent can be harmed, the gains from preventing that harm (which, at least in the eyes of those who will be suffering the loss, cannot be too great) are likely to be outweighed by the extra costs involved. Thus, if the utilitarian analysis is correct, the use of marijuana, for example, should not be a crime, either because the user is not harmed or because, if he is, he has judged that the gains to him outweigh that harm. In such cases, it is probable that the costs of administering the criminal justice system and of frustrating the desires of users outweigh any gains produced by preventing the drug from being used.

In general, the utilitarian analysis will lead to the same results as the harm principle. But there are exceptions to this. Two major types of exceptions are (a) cases in which administrative costs are too high and (b) cases in which the criminal fails to appreciate the loss he will suffer. Let's look at each of these in turn.

For the sake of discussion, suppose the prohibitionists are right in saying that alcohol use leads to a sufficient number of tragedies that the losses due to overuse outweigh any gains from moderate use. If this is so, then the harm principle says that the production and sale of alcohol should be made a crime, because it is an activity that results in a great harm. Nevertheless, as real experience shows, prohibiting something that a great many people want, and which they continue to use, is unlikely to be beneficial, because the cost of administering such laws is so great that it outweighs any gains. Thus, in this type of case, the utilitarian point of view disagrees with the harm principle.

The second exception involves the type of case that is well illustrated by usury laws. People who are willing to borrow money at usurious interest rates normally do so only when they are desperate. Under these circumstances, they are prone to the sort of misjudgments that lead them to accept loans that are highly disadvantageous to them. In these instances, the loss to the victim, even though he has consented to the action, is so great that the utilitarian analysis might well conclude that the gains from preventing usurious loans outweigh the costs of making them illegal. Thus, where the individual cannot adequately judge the full nature of the gains and losses to him, the utilitarian analysis may lead to different conclusions from those suggested by the harm principle.

We can now see how the utilitarian analysis offers us a definition of a crime. First, it states that the actions that should be made crimes are those for which the gains from stopping them outweigh the losses from stopping them. And, second, it says that the reason for making such actions crimes is that the consequences of doing so are beneficial, and we should always do that which leads to beneficial consequences. So here we have the utilitarian analysis as to *which* actions should be made crimes as well as a clear account of *why* we should make certain types of actions crimes.

4•3 A UTILITARIAN ANALYSIS OF THE CRIMINAL

According to the utilitarian, the whole goal of the criminal justice system is to deter criminals by threatening them with punishment. How does the threat of punishment work? The basic idea is very simple. Someone is contemplating committing a crime because he believes that the gains to him, monetary or otherwise, will outweigh the losses to him. The threat of punishment is supposed to change that calculation. If we have designed our criminal justice system properly, then the potential criminal will reevaluate his gains and losses and conclude that the losses from committing the crime (punishment) outweigh the gains, and he will be deterred.

What picture of the criminal is presupposed by this simple account of how deterrence works? Clearly, criminals are *not* seen as irrational beings given to peculiar forms of reasoning and uncontrolled behavior. On the contrary, they are viewed as people who think about things just the way you and I do. When deciding whether we should do something or not, we weigh the losses against the gains. The potential criminal, contemplating his criminal act, is doing the same thing. He is, in other words, simply trying to figure out whether it will pay for him to commit the crime. The goal of the criminal justice system is to change the circumstances sufficiently so that he will conclude that crime does *not* pay.

Notice that this picture of the potential criminal is entirely neutral as to the psychological or social forces operating on him. In fact, this picture is perfectly compatible with the view that it is the criminal's social circumstances that lead him to commit the crime and also with the view that it is the psychological forces in his upbringing that lead him to commit the crime. All that this picture requires is that the criminal be able to evaluate whether the crime will or will not pay. As long as such an evaluation can lead him to conclude that it will not pay to commit the crime, then there is a legitimate purpose for the criminal justice system. The utilitarian view of the criminal, therefore, is not troubled by those standard challenges to the criminal justice system we discussed in section 3.3. Utilitarians can accept the psychological and sociological determinism presupposed in those objections.

What about excuses and mitigations? Consider Jeremy Bentham's classical utilitarian account of a major excuse, insanity. The insane criminal, being insane, is not likely to be deterred by the threat of punishment. So there is nothing to gain by punishing him. But every punishment, from the utilitarian point of view, involves a loss, since the criminal suffers. Therefore, said Bentham, we should excuse insane criminals. In this way, Bentham tried to build a utilitarian theory in support of excuses and mitigations.

Unfortunately, Bentham's argument contains one major fallacy. Even if we agree that insane criminals will not be deterred by the threat of punishment, this does not mean that punishing an insane criminal has *no* deterrent effect. Why shouldn't it still help deter the criminal activities of those who are not insane? To begin with, if we punish all criminals, sane or insane, then there is a clear message to the sane potential criminal that he has no chance of getting away with a crime by finding an excuse or a mitigation. Second, the more criminals that we punish, the more seriously the threat of punishment will be taken. Therefore, even if the person who is punished has what we normally think of as a good excuse (such as insanity), his punishment is still justified in terms of its deterrent effect. The utilitarian theory of punishment leads to the conclusion that we ought to do away with excuses and mitigations. The reader will have to decide for himself whether this conclusion is acceptable.

Utilitarians are on firmer ground when they come to justifications. The whole point of a justification is to show why the action in question, while normally a crime, should not be a crime in this case. Utilitarian theory can accept justifications, but only for those acts which we want people to commit. Thus, if acts of self-defense, for example, are thought to lead to socially desirable consequences, then the utilitarian analysis we saw in section 4.2 will lead to the conclusion that these acts should not be crimes. And given that they are not crimes, we will not punish the person who performs them. The utilitarian problem, then, is with excuses and mitigations, not with justifications.

4·4 A UTILITARIAN ANALYSIS OF LEGAL PROCESSES

We saw in section 3.4 that there are two major value issues that must be dealt with when considering legal processes. The first is the relative importance of the goal of safeguarding innocent people from conviction and that of convicting the guilty. We saw the immediate implications of this issue for the question of what level of evidence to require for conviction: The more we are concerned with protecting the innocent, the higher the level of evidence we should require. The second issue concerns the type of techniques we can use for investigating crimes and apprehending suspects, including the procedural rights that suspects should have. Both these value issues arise in connection with the process of plea bargaining. In this section, we will see how utilitarians deal with these issues.

From the utilitarian point of view, the punishment of anyone, whether guilty or innocent, is bad. Thus, it is no worse to punish someone who is innocent than it is to punish someone who is guilty. However, since punishing someone who is known to be innocent does not deter criminals, whereas punishing someone who is known to be guilty does deter criminals, utilitarians, like everyone else, believe in punishing the guilty and not the innocent. If, though, we make a mistake and incorrectly judge someone to be guilty, the punishment he receives is viewed by the utilitarian as not much worse an evil than that received by the guilty. Moreover, as long as everyone thinks that the person is guilty, his punishment will have the same deterrent effect as it would if he were truly guilty.

This observation has staggering implications for our current system of criminal justice. It is widely known that there are many crimes for which no one is ever convicted and punished. As we have seen, one reason for this is the very strict requirements concerning evidence. Given that we need to prove guilt beyond all reasonable doubt, police often fail to arrest people they know are guilty but whose guilt they cannot prove, district attorneys often fail to bring people to trial for the same reason, and so on. As a result, the deterrent effect of the criminal justice system is lessened. Many criminals quite reasonably conclude that they can get away with their crime as long as they are careful. Suppose we were to lower the requirement, asking only that the *pre-ponderance* of evidence indicate guilt. Surely, many more crimes would be punished and the level of deterrence would go up. But, additionally, the number of innocent people who are convicted would also increase. So what? After all, as long as the level of evidence required is still reasonably high, people will continue to believe that these individuals are guilty and we will still get a deterrent effect from punishing them. And, from the utilitarian point of view, there is nothing that makes the punishment of the innocent much worse than the punishment of the guilty.

In short, if we hold the view that the suffering of a wrongfully punished person is very much worse than the suffering of a justly punished person, then we can make some sense of the current strict requirements for evidence. Furthermore, this belief allows us to understand why it is better that a thousand guilty people go unpunished (even if this leads to a great increase in crime) than that one innocent person be unjustly punished. If, however, we are utilitarians (who find nothing intrinsically right in punishing the guilty and have, therefore, great difficulty in thinking that punishing the innocent is much worse than punishing the guilty), then none of this makes sense. We should lower the amount of evidence required to a more reasonable standard — such as one which requires only that the preponderance of evidence point toward guilt — so that we would have far more convictions and thus see a substantial decrease in the level of crime. The reader will have to judge for himself whether this is a satisfactory suggestion.

The utilitarian point of view toward the question of procedural safeguards and due process of law is somewhat more complicated. Some of the procedural safeguards seem devoted to ensuring that the innocent are not mistakenly convicted. For example, the requirement that an attorney be present at all stages of the conviction process arose from the fact that, historically, when attorneys were not present, the police obtained more confessions—let us hope mistakenly, and not deliberately—from innocent parties than they did when attorneys were present. To the extent that procedural requirements are merely a way of trying to protect the innocent against wrongful conviction, they must be dealt with in a fashion similar to our analysis of what degree of evidence to require. Utilitarians might well want to modify the safeguard requirements to help produce a higher rate of conviction. There is, however, a different way of looking at *some* of these procedural requirements. Consider, for example, the requirement that the police not engage in illegal searches and seizures. This is a safeguard to protect people's privacy, especially the privacy of their homes. Dropping this requirement would create many undesirable consequences having nothing to do with the conviction of innocent people. People's sense of privacy and security in their homes would be disrupted. Therefore, from a utilitarian point of view, procedural requirements like the protection against illegal searches and seizures may well be justified.

In light of this argument, let's look at the institution of plea bargaining from a utilitarian perspective. As we explained earlier, plea bargaining is a form of negotiation in which a confession is obtained in return for a promise of a lower penalty. Plea bargaining has many desirable consequences: it lowers the costs of the criminal justice system by enabling many cases to be settled out of court, and it has a desirable deterrent effect by increasing the number of criminals convicted. Why, then, do people criticize plea bargaining? For one thing, it can lead to the conviction of some innocent people, those who, for one reason or another, plead guilty because they are afraid to go to trial. We already know that, from a utilitarian point of view, this is not such a powerful argument. Utilitarians are prepared to accept a somewhat higher incidence of wrongful punishment in exchange for a much larger increase in the deterrent effect. Other people object to plea bargaining on procedural grounds, arguing that it violates due process of law. But until they can show how this leads to other consequences that are sufficiently bad to outweigh the many advantages of plea bargaining, utilitarians must conclude that this institution should be retained.

4·5 A UTILITARIAN ANALYSIS OF PUNISHMENT

We saw in section 3.5 that one of the major problems with the criminal justice system today is the very uneven levels of punishment it metes out. The fact is that different crimes were introduced into the legal system at different times and no attempt has been made to create a system of punishment in which each type of crime is given an appropriate level of punishment as compared with other crimes.

One of the major strengths of the utilitarian analysis of punishment is that it offers us the possibility of creating a systematic scheme of punishment. In order to understand how it can do this, we must recall two fundamental points about the utilitarian approach:

1. It sees the criminal as a rational agent capable of figuring out whether it will pay for him to commit the crime he has in mind. Therefore, the minimum punishment for any given crime should be whatever is great enough to convince the potential criminal that it will *not* pay for him to commit the crime.

2. It views all punishment as a necessary evil. Therefore, we should not punish beyond what is needed to deter criminals. Thus, the minimum level of punishment will be identical to the maximum level of punishment.

These two basic points enable the utilitarian theorist to approach the question of how much punishment is appropriate for a given crime in a systematic fashion. To see how the theory works, suppose you must determine the appropriate punishment for someone who has stolen $100. You reason that a rational person would figure that crime pays if he can end up with any part of the stolen $100, and that crime does not pay if he loses anything in addition to the $100. Thus, you conclude that the appropriate punishment for stealing $100 is a fine of $100.01. This is sufficient to ensure that people will be deterred from committing the crime by seeing that the losses outweigh the gains, and it does not create unnecessary evil by exceeding that goal.

Unfortunately, the real world is much more complicated than our simple example indicates. To begin with, potential criminals know they have a good chance of getting away with their crime. In setting the level of punishment, therefore, you must take this fact into account. Suppose that only one in four criminals who steal $100 get caught and are punished. A fine of $100.01 will not deter a rational criminal who knows there is only a one in four chance he will be punished. We need to adjust the fine to compensate for the odds of getting caught. At $400.01, the punishment is just sufficient to convince the criminal that the theft will not pay.

Another complication is that in the real world there are many types of crimes for which it is difficult to estimate the exact gains and losses involved, thus making it much harder to calculate the penalties to set for them. Still, the basic formula is that: the penalty for committing a given crime multiplied by the probability of getting caught (the expected loss) should be minimally greater than the expected profit. In our example, the expected loss of $100.0025 ($400.01 × 0.25) is minimally greater than the expected gain of $100.

While this sort of calculation is very difficult to carry out in practice, the utilitarian approach to punishment does provide a convenient framework on which to base a rationale for assigning penalties. In sum, it states that the greater the gain for the criminal, all other things being equal, the higher we must set the penalty. And, the greater the probability of the criminal being caught, all other things being equal, the lower we may set the penalty.

Notice that in this determination of the proper level of punishment for a crime, the utilitarian point of view makes no consideration for the harm inflicted by the action. Remember, the goal of punishment for the utilitarian is to deter prospective criminals by making sure they realize that the crime they're contemplating will not pay. In order to arrive at this conclusion, the person has to take into account the potential gain, the possible punishment, and the probability of being punished. In deciding whether the crime pays for *him*, he is not concerned with the harm that will come to the victim. Therefore in trying to deter him, neither should *we* take this into account.

We are all aware that people do commit atrocious acts against others without seeming to gain anything by doing so. Many people feel instinctively that such criminals should be severely punished because of the great harm they inflict. As we have just seen, utilitarians disagree with this view. The reader must decide for himself which view is right and which wrong.

A second set of major moral issues that we raised in section 3.5 are those that concern what type of punishment to use. We pointed out that probation and imprisonment are among those most commonly employed, and their heavy use is being challenged by utilitarian analysts. These theorists argue that probation and imprisonment have the highly undesirable consequence of costing much more than they're worth. Systems of fines and/or corporeal punishment are a great deal cheaper to employ, and using them would free up society's resources for use on other, more valuable, projects. Therefore, utilitarians are seriously interested in doing away with the current emphasis on imprisonment and probation as the primary forms of criminal punishment.

The use of capital punishment is one of the most controversial issues pertaining to the criminal justice system. Let's assume (not unreasonably) that the death penalty is a more severe penalty from the criminal's point of view than are the alternatives, such as life imprisonment. Then, in the utilitarian framework, it follows that the death penalty should only be used when the alternatives are not sufficient to attain the desired level of deterrence.

This argument has led scholars to examine the data to see if capital punishment has a sufficiently greater deterrent impact over life imprisonment to justify its use. Most such studies have focused on the death penalty in connection with murders, since most proponents of the death penalty propose its use in that connection. Early studies, which compared the murder rate in states which employ the death penalty with that in states which have no death penalty, found no significant *additional* deterrent effect. Therefore, utilitarian theorists concluded that the death penalty was not justified. More recent investigations suggest that use of the death penalty does have a significant additional deterrent impact, but these studies are highly controversial. However, if they are upheld, utilitarians may well have to conclude that we should retain the death penalty.

4·6 CONCLUSIONS

In this chapter, we have examined one version of the utilitarian theory of the criminal justice system. Its basic idea is that the goal of this system is to deter certain types of behavior that we call crimes. An action should be made a crime if the costs of deterring it by use of the criminal justice system are less than the gains from making it a crime. The criminal is viewed as a self-interested rational agent who should not be excused for his crime. Legal processes should be modified so as to increase the probability that criminals will be punished, even if doing so causes a moderate increase in the number of innocent people punished. The level of punishment should be determined by the profit to the criminal and the probability of his getting caught, with the minimum (which is identical to the maximum) penalty set according to whatever is just sufficient to deter potential criminals. Prisons and probation should be deemphasized as the primary forms of punishment.

These are all highly controversial theses. Here, as elsewhere, utilitarianism is seen as a systematic approach that comes into conflict with some of our ordinary intuitions and common ways of doing things. In the next chapter we will see how the deontological point of view looks at these same issues.

Exercises

Define in your own words the following terms:

1. deterrence as the goal of criminal justice
2. the special deterrence/general deterrence distinction

3. the criminal as a rational agent
4. determinism
5. Bentham's theory of excuses
6. punishment as a necessary evil
7. the expected loss from committing a crime
8. the expected gain from committing a crime
9. additional deterrent effect of capital punishment

Review Questions

1. Why do utilitarians view the criminal justice system as a necessary evil?
2. What are the different ways in which punishment is supposed to deter people?
3. According to utilitarianism, which actions should be made crimes? How does this analysis compare with the harm principle?
4. What picture of the criminal is presupposed by the deterrence approach?
5. Why can the utilitarian accept without difficulty the idea that criminal actions are caused by psychological and sociological factors?
6. What is wrong with Bentham's theory of excuses and mitigations? Why can utilitarianism accommodate justifications better than excuses?
7. In what way does the utilitarian believe that there is nothing especially wrong with punishing the innocent? What are the implications of this belief?
8. What is the utilitarian theory of the ideal level of punishment?
9. How do utilitarians deal with the validity of capital punishment?

Questions for Further Thought

1. Should utilitarians add to their list of the beneficial consequences of punishment the notion that punishment satisfies the desires for vengeance on the part of the victim and his friends and/or family? If they do, what impact, if any, will this have on their approach to concrete questions about the criminal justice system?
2. Consider the conditions under which utilitarians believe in victimless crimes? To what extent does their position on this issue deal with the examples raised in Chapter 3?
3. Utilitarians are committed to a picture of the criminal as a rational agent. Does this view mean that the utilitarian theory only applies to "professional" criminals, or those capable of the sort of calcu-

lations described in the chapter? If not, how might it apply to other types of criminals as well?

4. Can Bentham's theory of excuses be saved, or must a contemporary utilitarian be thoroughly committed to doing away with excuses and mitigations?

5. Critically evaluate the following rebuttal to the utilitarian argument presented in section 4.4 of the chapter. "The argument presupposes that, from the utilitarian point of view, there is nothing especially wrong with punishing the innocent by mistake. But there is. When we punish someone who is innocent, we produce in the innocent victim an extra outrage. If we take that into account, utilitarianism has very different implications from those outlined in the text."

6. Is utilitarianism right in focusing on the relative deterrent impact of life imprisonment and capital punishment? Are there other unfavorable consequences of capital punishment which may lead to its exclusion by utilitarians, even if it does have a higher deterrent impact than life imprisonment?

Chapter Five

The Criminal Justice System: A Deontological Approach

In this chapter, we look at our moral questions relating to the criminal justice system from a deontological perspective. First, though, a word of caution: While nearly all deontologists agree on the basic theoretical framework that supports this approach to the criminal justice system, not all would agree on the detailed implications of that framework for the specific moral issues that concern us here. This chapter contains, therefore, *a* deontological approach to the criminal justice system, not *the only* deontological approach.

5·1 RETRIBUTION AS THE GOAL OF THE CRIMINAL JUSTICE SYSTEM

The fundamental idea behind the deontological approach to the criminal justice system is that the system is designed to meet the demands of retributive justice. To this end, it should punish those who have harmed people through violating their rights to an extent equivalent to the harm they have caused. Let's see just what this idea implies.

First, what do we mean by *retributive justice*? Basically, it is the idea that there is intrinsic good in punishing those who deserve to be punished, regardless of the consequences that might follow. If, for example, someone commits murder without justification, the murderer deserves to be punished and it is right that he be punished. Retributive justice is satisfied only when he receives an appropriate punishment.

It is extremely important to distinguish the goal of retributive justice from the goal of vengeance. Those who mistakenly equate the two tend to view believers in retributive justice as bloodthirsty members of a socially organized lynch mob. What is the distinction? Vengeance relates to the personal satisfaction one derives from seeing the criminal suffer for the crime he has committed. Retributive justice pertains to a commitment to see the criminal receive his just deserts. The main difference lies in the motivation behind the call for punishment. But there are other differences, too. Those who seek vengeance often punish far more severely than what is appropriate, and they may do so without taking sufficient care to ensure that it is the guilty party who is being punished. This is not surprising, for vengeance seekers want revenge for the wrong done, which is not the same as wanting justice. When a system of criminal justice is created to mete out what is demanded by retributive justice, it is easier to avoid the additional abuses that stem from the desire for vengeance. In short, the theory of retributive justice says that society should punish criminals to the extent that they receive what they deserve, but no more.

It should be immediately evident that there are a number of fundamental distinctions between this retributive approach and the deterrent approach discussed in Chapter 4. Believers in retributive justice accept the view that there is something intrinsically right about the suffering of the guilty when they are punished. Justice demands that they suffer for what they have done. In this respect, believers in retribution sharply disagree with the deterrent theorists' claim that punishment, even of the guilty, is a necessary evil justified only by its beneficial social consequences. In addition, believers in retribution see punishment as essentially backward-looking while believers in deterrence see it as essentially forward-looking. For supporters of deterrence, the justification of punishment is put in terms of its future beneficial consequences. In this way, believers in deterrence are looking at the future. Believers in retribution justify punishment as an appropriate response to what has been done in the past. In this way, their view of punishment is backward-looking.

Naturally, believers in the retributive approach to the criminal justice system are well aware that a beneficial social consequence of that system is its deterrent effect. They have no objection to this additional benefit, but they are clear in stating that this is not the purpose of punishment. Here is what they say on the subject:

1. However beneficial this deterrence effect may be, it is not what justifies the use of punishment. If the person punished didn't deserve the punishment, the deterrent impact wouldn't justify the punishment.
2. In structuring the criminal justice system, we should design it in light of the goal of retribution, not in light of the goal of deterrence.

As we shall see in the rest of this chapter, the retributive approach, as outlined in these two points, leads to quite different conclusions about the criminal justice system than those which stem from the deterrence approach.

One final point. It is sometimes claimed that believers in the retributive approach to punishment are fanatics about seeing that all criminals are punished. Even some believers in this approach agree with the claim, suggesting that if a society were breaking up, so that its punishments could have no deterrent impact, one of its last acts should still be to punish all those guilty parties not yet punished. This is sheer extremism.

From the retributive point of view, the goal of the criminal justice system is to exact a certain type of justice. This is an important goal, but society will have to expend many resources in order to meet it. We have other legitimate goals, and they, too, make demands on society's resources. Any balanced social theory will have to take into account the many demands for resources imposed by a wide variety of goals and allocate to each goal an appropriate share of social resources. In short, a society which is in the process of breaking up may find that there are numerous legitimate demands that will surely take precedence over that of punishing any remaining unpunished criminals. By the same token, a flourishing society may refrain from punishing some guilty parties because the cost of doing so is too great and the resources could be better used elsewhere.

With this background to the basic idea behind the retributive theory of punishment, we will spend the rest of the chapter exploring this idea more fully as we see its implications for our moral problems.

5·2 A DEONTOLOGICAL THEORY OF THE DEFINITION OF A CRIME

Our first moral issue concerning the criminal justice system was the question of which actions the legislature should declare illegal. The quick deontological answer is that any action which harms people by violating their rights should be illegal. Let's see just what this means.

The deontologist maintains that two conditions must be satisifed before an action can legitimately be made a crime: (1) it must harm people and (2) it must violate their rights. In addition, as we saw at the end of section 5.1, deontologists will object to making an action a crime unless a third condition is satisfied: (3) the extra resources required to enforce and prosecute this new crime must not be needed to meet some other, more urgent, social objective.

The first thing to note about these sets of conditions is that they are neutral on the question of victimless crimes. Let's see what a deontologist might say about aiding a suicide, for example. Some deontologists would argue that aiding someone who commits suicide should be a crime because that act harms the person whose life is lost and violates his right to life, even though the suicide victim obviously has consented to the aid. Thus, some deontologists are willing to accept the notion of victimless crimes. Other deontologists, however, challenge this analysis. Their crucial point is that in all such cases there can be no violation of the rights of the party who is harmed. The suicide victim, by consenting to the aid, has waived his right to life. In sum, this alternative deontological approach claims that a person can waive any particular right, and then no one can be punished for violating that right. By this reasoning, there can be no legitimate cases of victimless crimes.

The second thing to note about these conditions is that they show the way in which the deontological approach differs from the harm principle. To begin with, there will be many cases in which an action may harm other people yet the deontologist will reject the claim that it should be made a crime on the grounds that the action has not violated anyone's rights. Recall, for example, Chapter 3's case, in which my competing grocery store causes harm to you by taking away some of your customers. The deontologist will reject any claim that such competitive behavior should be made criminal. There is no right which entitles anyone to be free from competition. Therefore, since I have not violated any of your rights by opening my store, I have not committed a crime.

Going back to our example from Chapter 4, deontologists will also reject any claim that the production and sale of alcohol should be a crime, even if it is shown that alcohol abuse is quite harmful. The reason for their rejection of prohibition laws relates to the third condition, which (based on real experience with prohibition) indicates that the extra resources needed to support such a law should be used to meet other, more pressing, objectives. In short, then, the deontological theory of criminal actions is able to avoid many of the weaknesses of the harm principle.

We have been discussing the question of which actions should be made crimes. We saw in Chapter 3 that any satisfactory theory that seeks to answer this question must also explain *why* those actions should be made crimes. After all, making some action a crime and punishing people for performing it are forms of coercion, and the use of coercion requires a justification.

The deontological theory offers a very simple explanation: The use of coercion is justified by society's obligation to protect people's rights. This feature of deontological thinking distinguishes this approach from all other theories on this issue. To illustrate, consider an action which clearly violates the rights of others, like murder. The deontologist says that precisely because murder violates the rights of another person, society may legitimately use coercion to prevent it. Furthermore, the potential murderer can hardly complain that society is coercing him into not violating someone's right to life, since committing this violation is not something that he may legitimately do in the first place. Thus, because the deontologist requires that all crimes involve the violation of rights, he has no difficulty justifying making such actions crimes.

5·3 A DEONTOLOGICAL ANALYSIS OF THE CRIMINAL

We saw in section 3.3 that any adequate theory of the criminal justice system must provide an analysis of the criminal which does at least two things: (1) give us an account of which are the legitimate excuses, mitigations, and justifications and (2) enable us to deal with the fundamental challenge to the criminal justice system that no person should ever be punished. Utilitarianism, as we saw in section 4.3, does provide us with such a theory of the criminal. It says that, in at least some circumstances, we should do away with excuses and mitigations but keep justifications. In this way, as long as the criminal's behavior can still be modified by the threat of punishment, the criminal justice system need not be concerned with the psychological and social forces operating on him. Let's see how this approach compares with the way the deontological theory of retributive justice looks at these issues.

The fundamental theme in the retributive analysis of the criminal is the notion that only a person who is responsible for a crime should be punished. Those who are not responsible for their behavior should not be punished, even if they cause harm to others by violating their rights. Justice is served only when these criteria are satisfied.

On this premise, it is relatively easy to anticipate the retributive stance on excuses and mitigations. In the case of excuses, such as insanity or being too young or lacking an intention, the criminal does not deserve to be punished because he is not responsible for what he did. In the case of mitigations, the criminal is only partially responsible for his behavior and therefore deserves only a partial penalty.

Modern utilitarians, who reject excuses and mitigations, argue that it pays to punish even those criminals who are traditionally excused because punishing them will have a deterrent impact on other criminals. Believers in the retributive theory of punishment can easily accept the fact that punishing these people will have a deterrent impact, but they still argue against punishment. They maintain that a person who is not responsible for his actions does not deserve to be punished and therefore should not be punished. The fact that punishing him will have a deterrent impact on others does not justify punishing him. This helps clarify our earlier statement that believers in retribution see deterrence only as a side benefit that cannot be allowed to shape the functioning of the criminal justice system. Thus, when retributive justice does not demand punishment, believers in retribution will not punish, even though doing so may have some deterrent impact.

Let's now look at justifications from the retributive perspective, using the case of self-defense as an example. When I take the life of someone who is trying to kill me, I have not, according to the retributive point of view, violated any of that person's rights. Roughly speaking, by virtue of attempting to kill me, in a manner that leaves me no other way to save myself, the person has forfeited his right to life. Therefore, my action is justified and I should not be punished by the criminal justice system. Remember, from the point of view of the retributive approach, nothing should be a crime unless it involves the violate of someone's rights.

The themes of responsibility and violation of rights supply a logical foundation for the deontological theory of excuses, mitigations, and justifications. However, this approach runs into serious difficulties when faced with the psychological and social determination views of human behavior. The source of that difficulty lies in the following structure.

1. Suppose that the criminal's behavior is caused by psychological and social forces operating on him.
2. If this is so, he is not responsible for his criminal acts.
3. Therefore, he should not be punished by the criminal justice system.

The utilitarian approach has no difficulty with this argument because it denies the legitimacy of the move from (2) to (3). It says that as long as the threat of punishment can deter people from committing crimes, then criminals should be punished even if they are not responsible for their actions. This easy way out is not open to deontologists who adopt the retributive approach. In claiming that responsibility is a requisite for legitimate punishment, they must accept the move from (2) to (3). If they want to reject the determination approach, all they can do is deny the truth of (1) or claim that (1) does not lead to (2).

Both these options have been adopted by believers in the retributive theory. Those who deny the truth of (1) claim that while psychological and social factors (upbringing and environment) may dispose people toward criminal behavior, any individual is still free to choose whether or not to be a criminal. Only those, like the insane, whose actions are caused by their delusions, are not responsible and should not be punished. In short, these deontologists (whom we call *indeterminists*) deny the claim that the behavior of the normal criminal is caused by psychological and social factors. Indeterminists believe that the behavior of normal criminals, and of normal people in general, is primarily the result of their own free choice.

Other supporters of the retributive theory reject the determination approach by denying the move from (1) to (2). While accepting the claim that the behavior of criminals is caused by psychological and social forces, they argue that this causality is nevertheless compatible with viewing the criminal as responsible for his actions. These theorists, called *compatibilists*, defend this view by reinterpreting the definition of responsibility. One standard version of the compatibilist explanation runs as follows: Someone is responsible for his behavior, even if his choice is dictated by outside forces, as long as he is satisfied and happy with his choices and behavior. Therefore, the ordinary criminal, if he is perfectly satisfied and happy with his choice to commit crimes, is responsible for his actions and deserves to be punished, even though his choices may be determined by outside forces.

According to compatibilists, then, a criminal is not responsible only in those cases where he is compelled to act in ways that make him unhappy and dissatisfied. However, the ordinary criminal, who is perfectly satisfied with his choice, is responsible and deserves to be punished even if his choice is caused.

In summary, deontologists who believe in the retributive approach to criminal justice have two different models of the criminal. On one, the criminal's behavior is caused by his freely made choices; while psychological and social forces may influence this choice, they do not cause it. On the second model, the criminal's choices and actions are caused by these forces, but the criminal is nevertheless responsible for his actions. Either model of the criminal offers an explanation of why we have excuses, mitigations, and justifications.

5·4 A DEONTOLOGICAL ANALYSIS OF LEGAL PROCESSES

As we saw in sections 3.4 and 4.4, there are two major value questions that must be dealt with when considering legal processes. One is the relative importance of the goal of safeguarding innocent people from conviction and that of convicting the guilty. The other concerns the procedural rights that suspects should have during the process of criminal investigation. Both these issues, as we have noted, arise in connection with the practice of plea bargaining.

We will see here that this is an area in which the deontological approach (based on the theory of retributive justice) differs significantly from the utilitarian approach (based on the concept of deterrence). To begin to understand why, we need to take another look at the way each of these theories views punishment, both the punishment of the guilty and the mistaken punishment of the innocent.

As we saw in section 4.4, utilitarian theorists find punishment (even of the guilty) an evil, although one that is justified. From their point of view, punishing the guilty and punishing the innocent are equally bad; the only difference is that the former evil is justified by its deterrent impact while the latter evil is not. Because of this, and because the mistaken punishment of innocent people who are believed guilty has the same deterrent impact, utilitarian theorists who emphasize deterrence are prepared to change the legal processes in ways that will help convict many more criminals, even at the cost of increasing the number of innocent people who are mistakenly punished.

This whole matter is analyzed quite differently by the retributivists, who find the utilitarian approach morally offensive. According to these theorists, the social benefit that is obtained by punishing people cannot by itself justify such punishment. After all, when someone is punished, he is being deprived of many of his fundamental rights, and we cannot deprive people of these rights just because we find it socially useful to do so. To retributivists, the only justification for depriving people of their rights is that the person deserves to be punished.

This same point of view leads to the belief that if we mistakenly punish someone who is innocent, we are doing a great wrong. We have, without any justification, seriously infringed upon the rights of an innocent party. Remember, retributivists do not consider the deterrent effect a sufficient justification for punishment; so, while it may have some deterrent impact, the mistaken punishment of an innocent party is a far more serious matter from the retributivist point of view than it is from the deterrent point of view. Thus, the deterrent theorists can accept with some equanimity a moderate increase in the number of innocent people mistakenly punished, but the retributive theorists must find this result highly objectionable.

All this has tremendous impact for the question of what degree of evidence we should require before someone can be convicted of a crime. Currently, our society employs the relatively stringent standard of proof beyond any reasonable doubt. We saw in section 4.4 that utilitarianism, with its emphasis on deterrence, leads to the conclusion that this requirement should be lowered. Doing so will no doubt result in some increase in the number of innocent people punished, but this is acceptable from the utilitarian point of view. Yet, for the reasons we have just seen, it is not acceptable from the retributive point of view. Therefore, deontologists, who accept the retributive approach, advocate the continued maintenance of our current strict requirements on evidence.

What we have seen so far also has significant implications for the question of procedural safeguards and due process of law. Some of these requirements seem designed to protect the innocent, such as that which says an attorney must be present at all stages of the process. Utilitarians, as we saw in section 4.4, might well be prepared to do away with, or in any case to modify, the stringency of these procedural safeguards, because they are willing to accept a somewhat higher rate of conviction for innocent parties. Deontologists, as we have just seen, are not prepared to accept this; therefore, they are in favor of maintaining these procedural safeguards.

We come, finally, to the question of plea bargaining. We have seen that the critics of plea bargaining object to it either on the grounds that it is an unfair process, even if applied to the guilty, or because it sometimes produces confessions from innocent people. These types of concerns are shared by all deontologists. Therefore, unlike the utilitarians, deontologists are opposed to plea bargaining. In the following section we will see that deontologists have another, even more fundamental, objection to plea bargaining.

5·5 A DEONTOLOGICAL ANALYSIS OF PUNISHMENT

We know from earlier discussions that a major problem with our current system of criminal justice is the very uneven levels of punishment it metes out. Some crimes seem to be punished with disproportionately high penalties while others carry disproportionately low penalties. A strength of the utilitarian analysis, which we saw in section 4.5, is that it provides the basis for creating a rational scheme of punishment. The penalty for committing a given type of crime, multiplied by the probability of getting caught, should be minimally greater than the profit from committing that crime.

Deontologists have an alternative analysis, which also provides a systematic basis for creating a schedule of punishment for different crimes. Deontologists feel that the utilitarian analysis leaves out the most important aspect that one should consider in setting the punishment—the harm caused by the criminal. To illustrate why deontologists attach so much importance to the harm and suffering that result from a crime, consider the following case. A group of teenagers break into the home of an old and poor person. They tie and gag him and then steal his few possessions. They leave without untying him, and he subsequently dies from lack of food and water.

Now the gain to the criminals in this case is very small. So the punishment, even taking into account that such criminals are not often caught, need not be very high in order to deter potential crimes of this nature. But deontologists are concerned with something other than deterrence. Our sense of retributive justice, they claim, tells us that these criminals should be punished severely because of the great harm they inflicted on their elderly victim. Deontologists conclude that we need a theory of punishment based on retributive justice, not on deterrence.

It is this same feeling about retributive justice that lies behind the deontologist's final objection to the institution of plea bargaining. As a result of plea bargaining, many criminals who commit serious crimes which inflict great harm on others are allowed to plead guilty to lesser charges and given only moderate penalties. This offends our sense of retributive justice, says the deontologist. Therefore, to the greatest extent possible, we must try to avoid the use of plea bargaining, even if it is justified from a deterrent point of view.

So far, we have used examples in which the deontologist would punish criminals more severely than would the deterrence proponents. But there are some cases in which the deontologist would conclude that the deterrence analysis overpunishes. Consider, for example, a crime which inflicts only a moderate amount of harm on others.

Moreover, suppose it is one that is difficult to detect, so the probability of getting caught and being punished for it is quite low. If we are to create a proper deterrent effect, we would have to assign a very severe penalty to the crime, way out of proportion to the harm it causes. The deterrence analysis would probably have to accept this conclusion. Deontologists, however, would reject it as being unfair to the criminal. The only acceptable way to deal with this problem from the deontological point of view is to take measures which increase the probability of detecting the crime.

In sum, deontologists feel that the utilitarian analysis of the level of punishment, while systematic, is wrong because it fails to focus on the crucial element—the harm that the criminal has caused others. Deontologists put forward as their own systematic theory the view that we should punish criminals to an extent equivalent to the harm they have caused. In this way, they put the focus on the proper element in determining the right level of punishment.

This leads us directly to the question of the type of punishment that should be employed. Earlier versions of the retributive theory seemed to suggest that the only truly equivalent punishment was one that did to the criminal the same thing that he did to his victim. This was the literal meaning of "an eye for an eye." But putting this theory into practice leads to some obvious difficulties: How, for example, are we to punish the degenerate rapist of an innocent child? In any case, modern retributive theory does not require "an eye for an eye." The typical victim of a crime has suffered a certain loss. Justice demands only that we inflict an *equivalent* loss on the criminal, not an *identical* loss. Since we want to do this with the least cost to society, retributivists as well as utilitarians are interested in exploring alternatives to the expensive system of imprisonment and/or probation.

Perhaps the only exception to this rejection of imposing identical losses is in connection with the death penalty for murderers. It is difficult to see from the retributive point of view what penalty of less severity than death could punish a murderer to the same extent that he has harmed his victim. So, believers in the retributive approach to punishment are inclined to support the death penalty. They do so simply because the death penalty seems to be the only way to satisfy the demands of retributive justice.

5·6 CONCLUSIONS

In this chapter we have examined a deontological theory of the criminal justice system. The basic idea behind this approach is that the goal of the criminal justice system is to exact retributive justice by punishing criminals to an extent equivalent to the harm they have caused. An action may be considered a crime only if it harms people through violating their rights. On one model, the criminal is a responsible agent because his actions are not caused, and on another model because his actions are not compelled. Criminals that do not fit these models should be excused for their crimes. Legal processes should continue to emphasize protection for those who are mistakenly accused of crimes, even if this increases the number of guilty parties who escape punishment. Plea bargaining should be abolished to the greatest extent possible; this is part of the process of restoring the view that the level of punishment should depend upon the amount of harm caused.

These are highly controversial theses, many of which are in direct conflict with the theses that follow from the utilitarian emphasis on deterrence. We conclude this section on criminal justice, therefore, with the observation that it is absolutely essential that we make up our mind as to what we want as our basic goal for the criminal justice system. Until this value question is resolved, we cannot decide how to structure that system.

Exercises

Define in your own words the following terms:

1. retributive justice
2. vengeance
3. waive a right
4. responsibility
5. indeterminists
6. compatibilists
7. retributive theory of the amount of punishment

Review Questions

1. What is the main goal of the criminal justice system according to our deontological analysis? How does that goal differ from the desire for vengeance?
2. What are the main differences between the deterrent theory and the retributive theory?

3. What does the deontological theory say about which actions should be made crimes? How does it differ from the harm principle? What does it say about victimless crimes?

4. How do believers in retributive justice explain the existence of excuses and mitigations?

5. What is the major difference between indeterminism and compatibilism? What are the strengths and weaknesses of each approach?

6. Why are retributivists so insistent upon not punishing the innocent? What are the implications of this insistence?

7. What is the retributive theory of the ideal level of punishment? How does it differ from the deterrence theory's approach to this question?

8. How do retributivists deal with the validity of capital punishment?

Questions for Further Thought

1. How does the retributive notion of justice compare with such notions of justice as giving someone back his property which you took by mistake, or giving someone his fair share of the rewards of a common enterprise?

2. Critically evaluate the views on both sides of the debate as to whether (a) all rights can be waived, and (b) there can be, from a retributive point of view, any victimless crimes.

3. What does the retributivist mean when he talks about people being responsible for their actions? Would indeterminists and compatibilists answer that question differently?

4. Critically evaluate the following objection: "Retributivists, by maintaining the current high standards for both evidence and due process, are advocating a criminal justice system with a low deterrence rate. This means that the rights of many more innocent victims will be infringed upon by undeterred criminals. How can retributivists, who are such strong believers in the rights of individuals, accept this?"

5. Is it correct to focus only on the harm caused by the criminal in setting his punishment? If a criminal can gain a lot by causing only a modest harm to his victim, is it right to encourage him to do so by setting a low level of punishment?

6. The argument in section 5.5 presupposes that only the death penalty punishes the murderer to the same extent as he has harmed his victim. Is this assumption accurate? What about those cases in which murderers seem to prefer death to life imprisonment?

Chapter Six

Value Problems Concerning the Distribution of Wealth

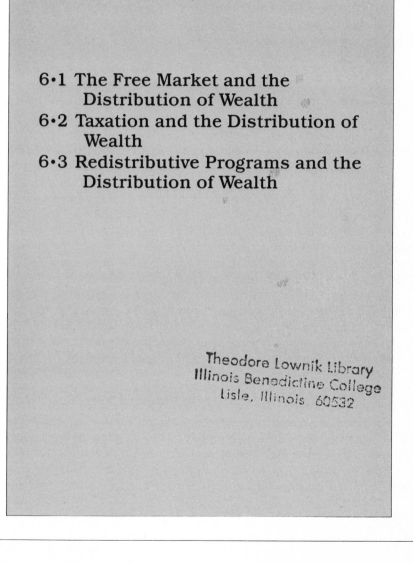

6·1 The Free Market and the Distribution of Wealth

6·2 Taxation and the Distribution of Wealth

6·3 Redistributive Programs and the Distribution of Wealth

The second set of moral issues with which we will be concerned relates to the distribution of wealth in America. There are few who would maintain that wealth is something that carries intrinsic value. At the same time, few would deny that wealth has considerable value for the many things it enables us to obtain. Those who have adequate wealth are able to satisfy many of their desires; those without adequate wealth are unable to satisfy many of their desires. So the way wealth is distributed among people is a matter of great interest and concern; it also poses a great many value questions for which each of us must find answers.

One of the fundamental features of a society is that, generally, wealth is distributed unequally among its members. Some people have a great deal of wealth while others have very little. *Egalitarians* are people who view this disparity as unfair. They believe that wealth should be distributed much more equally than it is in most societies. One of the fundamental value questions with which we shall be concerned is whether this egalitarian attitude is justified, and, if it is, how much equality should we strive for and how should we go about getting it.

A second fundamental value problem concerning the distribution of wealth is that people's wealth is not closely correlated with the effort they make, or with the contribution they make, or with their moral integrity. Some good people work very hard and make important contributions yet have only a modest amount of wealth while others work very little and contribute nothing of merit and have a great deal of wealth. *Meritocrats* are people who feel that wealth should be distributed in proportion to individual merit to a much greater extent than it is in most societies. So the second major value question we will consider is whether the meritocratic feeling is justified, and, if so, what social steps should we take to realize the meritocratic ideal. It is important to recognize that meritocracy is in direct opposition to egalitarianism. After all, given two people of unequal merit, the egalitarian will treat them much more equally than will the meritocrat. We will examine each approach in detail in the two following chapters.

In this chapter, we will develop a basic understanding of the processes which determine the distribution of wealth in America today. As we shall see, these processes raise still further value questions about the distribution of wealth. Moreover, a close look at them will lead us to some insights about the big questions of egalitarianism and meritocracy. Each feature of the system through which wealth is distributed in the United States will be examined separately, and value questions concerning each aspect will be raised at the appropriate points.

6·1 THE FREE MARKET AND THE DISTRIBUTION OF WEALTH

One of the fundamental systems by which wealth is distributed in America is through the operations of the free market economy, which involves private ownership of property and free exchanges between people. Let's see how this system works to distribute wealth.

At any given time in our society, a large amount of the wealth is owned by private individuals. Some of this wealth is used to purchase goods and services, like food, shelter, clothing, and so forth. Some of it is hidden away in mattresses, bank vaults, and other such locations. Most of it, however, is invested. Wealth can be invested in any number of ways, but the goal is always that it will earn more wealth for its owner. Thus, people deposit money in a bank, buy bonds, give mortgages, and so forth with the expectation that loaning their money will earn them more money (interest). People also invest in stocks, hoping, among other things, to earn good dividends from them. Or, they might use their money as capital, investing in their businesses with the expectation of making greater profits. At any given time, then, much of society's wealth is being used by private individuals to obtain more wealth.

Of course not all societies have as extensive a system of private enterprise as ours. In many societies, the only goods that may be privately owned are consumer items, such as food, clothing, and household furnishings. All other goods and services are owned by the state. In these societies, one cannot accumulate wealth and use it as a source of income. Since the ownership of all means of production is in the hands of the state, one cannot buy shares in businesses. And the practice of lending money at interest does not exist.

Many questions can be raised concerning the respective merits and demerits of private ownership of nonconsumer goods (often called the means of production) and of the use of accumulated wealth as a means of earning more wealth. However, it is not within the scope of this book to address all these issues. For instance, we do not seek to compare alternative economic systems. Instead, our aim is to explore the value questions concerning our own system's methods of distributing wealth.

Since our system allows those who have accumulated wealth to accumulate even more wealth through interest, dividends, and profits, one of the value questions which we consider in this book is whether this practice is desirable. The following two chapters explore this issue at length from both the utilitarian and deontological perspectives. At this point we should only note that both egalitarians and meritocrats have problems with this use of accumulated wealth to obtain still further wealth. Egalitarians object to this practice on the grounds that it leads to even greater disparities in the distribution of wealth. The rich get richer while the poor get proportionally poorer. Meritocrats object to this practice to the extent that such accumulated wealth may be inherited. Since the owner of inherited wealth has not accumulated his money through merit, any money he earns from this wealth is undeserved from a meritocratic point of view. Similarly, meritocrats are concerned that private ownership of productive resources leads to a less meritocratic distribution of wealth.

We mentioned earlier that our free market system relies on free exchanges among individuals. One of the most important examples of this is the labor contract. Those who own and control the means of production hire laborers for a period of time in return for an agreed-upon wage. These laborers use the means of production to produce products that are sold to other people in return for an agreed-upon price. These freely made agreements play an important role in determining the distribution of wealth in our society, for those who reach favorable agreements become wealthier while those who make unfavorable agreements get poorer.

All this gives rise to still another fundamental set of value questions: Can we count on these free exchanges to be fair? If so, why? If not, should we continue to accept the distribution of wealth brought about through these agreements?

An example should help clarify the implications of these questions. Many people feel that certain members of the work force are paid too little for the work they do. They argue that these workers agree to such low wages only because they have no other choices. The person who hires them benefits from their labor and from the low wages he is paying while the workers receive far less than they deserve. Those who hold this view conclude that this practice unfairly yields great profit to the employer and that we should not allow it.

It is this type of reasoning that lies behind the minimum wage laws. In passing these laws, we are saying, in effect, that we will not accept the implications for the distribution of wealth that come from people's willingness to work at too low a wage. There are others, however, who object to this line of reasoning and to the minimum wage laws. While there are many very different arguments for opposing the minimum wage, at least some of those objectors claim that rational adults should be entitled to reach any agreement they choose to, and it is not society's place to police or to prevent some of those agreements.

To summarize, the distribution of wealth in America is largely determined by private ownership of the means of production and by free exchanges among individuals. These features of our economic system raise important value questions: Should there be private ownership of the means of production, along with the corollary assumption that an individual can use accumulated wealth to obtain still further wealth? Should we allow all freely agreed-upon exchanges among adults, even if they enable the rich to get richer at the expense of others? We will be looking at these value questions in the next two chapters, both on their own and in connection with the theories of egalitarianism and meritocracy.

One final point: America's current economic system contains many elements besides private ownership and free exchange among people. We will be talking about some of them (for instance, taxation and redistribution of wealth) in the following sections. We will see that, despite America's very strong stand in favor of private property and free exchanges, we do place certain limits on the rights of the private owner and on conditions under which goods may be freely exchanged. These limits bear testimony to the fact that there are many doubts about absolute private ownership and unrestrained free exchange. It is hoped that our discussion of these issues in this and the next two chapters will help resolve some of these doubts.

6·2 TAXATION AND THE DISTRIBUTION OF WEALTH

In addition to the free market system, another institution that plays a major role in the distribution of wealth in America is the government, both on the federal and local levels. By taking money from us in the form of taxes and giving it back by spending money on various programs, the government serves as a redistributor of wealth. In this section we will look at the taxation portion of this process. Then in the next section, we will look at the redistribution side of the process.

Any system of taxation has to deal with two major questions. The first is the choice of the *tax base* — that is, the choice as to what is to be taxed. The second is the choice of the amount, or the percentage, to be taxed for each unit of this base, the choice of the *tax rate*.

Some simple examples will clarify these concepts. Imagine a society in which every person is taxed $100/year. In this case, the tax base is the individual person, since the tax is applied to each person, and the rate is $100, since each unit of the base is taxed at that amount. Now imagine a society in which everyone is taxed a fixed percentage of their wealth, say 5 percent. Here, the tax base is wealth, and the rate of taxation is 5 percent.

Both these choices raise value questions. Are there any moral reasons for preferring one tax base to another? Are there any moral reasons for preferring one rate of taxation to another? A look at the current system of taxation as practiced in America will shed some light on these questions.

In America today there are three different bases for taxation. One is income. Income taxes — including personal income taxes, corporate income taxes, and social security taxes — constitute the major source of revenue for the federal government. Income taxes also provide revenue for state and local governments, although to a lesser degree. A second base for taxation is people's expenditures. State and local sales taxes are the most prominent examples. In addition to the general sales tax, we have a variety of special taxes on such goods as gasoline, cigarettes, liquor, and luxury items. The third base for taxation is wealth. One important example of this is the property tax imposed by local governments.

An interesting hybrid tax is the estate tax, which taxes inheritances. Some people prefer to think of this as a tax on wealth which is levied only at the time the owner of the wealth dies. Others prefer to think of it as an expenditure tax, which taxes the purchase of wealth for one's heirs. We will see in the following chapters that this subtle disagreement greatly affects the ways in which we think about inheritance in general and inheritance taxes in particular.

Some people claim that an appropriate and fair tax is one that is based on expenditures. They say that the purchase of consumer goods and services uses up some of society's resources, and people should be taxed on the basis of their consumption of those resources. Others claim that the fair and proper basis for taxation is wealth. Wealth is correlated with ability to pay; the more wealth one has, the more one is able to pay without suffering a disproportionate loss. Still another group claims that income is the most appropriate base for taxation. They, too, believe that people should be taxed according to their ability to pay. But they argue that income, not wealth, is the best measure of one's ability to pay, because even if a person has some wealth, he does not have much ability to pay if that wealth is not generating income.

It should be clear that the choice of a tax base is really a choice between competing views of fairness and justice, and that the choice of different tax bases has different implications for the degree of equality and meritocracy we will have in our society. Therefore, the choice of a tax base is not a purely economic decision, and any proper moral theory on the distribution of wealth must address the issues surrounding this question.

Tax rates generally can be classified in three categories: proportional, progressive, and regressive. A *proportional tax* rate is one that taxes each unit of the tax base at the same amount, or at the same percentage. Sales taxes are proportional taxes, because every item of expenditure is taxed the same percent. A *progressive tax* rate is a tax rate in which additional units are taxed at a higher rate than earlier units. In theory, at least, the personal income tax is a progressive tax, because the tax rate rises for higher income levels. The third type of tax rate is a *regressive tax*. Here, the additional units are taxed at a lower rate than earlier units. The social security tax is an example, since earnings above a certain level (currently $32,400) are exempt from this tax.

The value implications of the choice between a progressive, proportional, or regressive rate of taxation are just as powerful as those concerning the choice of a tax base. Egalitarians, for example, greatly prefer progressive rates on a tax base of either income or wealth. Their reasoning is that progressive rates, as opposed to proportional rates, increase the amount of money paid to the government by those who have the most income or wealth. In this way, society's wealth can be distributed more equally and, thus, more fairly. Meritocrats, on the other hand, oppose progressive tax rates, particularly on a tax base of income. They claim that such taxes penalize those who are successful by taking money away from those who deserve it. So, meritocrats often prefer proportional taxes. Others object to progressive tax rates on the grounds that everyone should be taxed equally and that it is unfair to tax some income or wealth at a higher rate than other income or wealth. Again, you can see that these questions are not purely economic.

To summarize, the American system of taxation employs three major tax bases (income, expenditures, and wealth) and three types of tax rates (progressive, proportional, and regressive). This complicated mix is obviously not the result of any well-thought-out general approach to taxation. Consequently, we are faced with some serious value questions, because our views about equality, fairness, and merit should play a fundamental role in shaping our tax scheme. In the next two chapters we will see how the adoption of systematic moral theories can help clarify these important value questions.

6·3 REDISTRIBUTIVE PROGRAMS AND THE DISTRIBUTION OF WEALTH

The government uses its tax revenue to finance a wide variety of programs, some of which are designed to redistribute the nation's wealth. In this section we will examine the nature of these redistributive programs to see how they work and to see why they pose value questions for us.

Many government programs provide goods and services to all citizens, or at least to all who want them, without regard to individual circumstances, such as financial need. Examples include national defense, the post office, interstate highways, national parks, and so forth. Similar programs on the state and local levels include police and fire protection, public education, libraries, highways, and other things. While provision of some of these goods and services could be left to the free market system, for one reason or another we choose to provide them through the government. Because they are provided equally to all citizens, regardless of the amount of taxes one pays, these programs produce at least some redistribution of wealth.

This last point often goes unnoticed, so it deserves a more careful explanation. Suppose you are the head of a family of four and earning an income of $12,000 a year. At this income, your tax payments are quite modest; they certainly do not cover the cost of educating your two children, for example. Let's assume that it costs $3,000/year per child to buy that education privately and that you would be willing to pay that amount if you had the money to do so. In effect, then, the government program of public education increases your wealth by $6,000 a year by providing you a service that costs that much and that is worth that much to you. So providing services is one way that tax revenue is used to redistribute wealth.

Other types of government programs are more explicitly redistributive in nature. Income security and welfare programs are designed expressly for people who, in one way or another, are in need of financial aid. These programs redistribute wealth from one group of citizens to another: from the nonpoor to the poor (welfare programs), from the employed to the unemployed (unemployment insurance), from the young to the old (social security), and so on. These programs are extremely widespread in scope. In fiscal year 1982, 34 percent of all government spending, or nearly $240 billion, went to finance this type of aid. Clearly, the adoption of such programs is a major commitment on the part of society to redistribute wealth from those who have more to those who have less.

In sum, almost all government programs succeed in redistributing society's wealth. Some are explicitly designed for this purpose — income security and welfare programs — while others achieve this result indirectly — national defense, education, etc. There are many questions that are commonly raised about these redistributive programs. The most prominent are discussed below.

The Legitimacy of Redistributive Programs. Throughout the ages, people with means have voluntarily come to the aid of those in need. Private charity is as old as human history. But the programs we have been discussing are not a part of this tradition. To begin with, there is nothing voluntary about them. They are funded by mandatory taxes which the government collects from everyone and uses in the manner it considers most appropriate, regardless of the taxpayer's interest in helping the needy. Second, the government, not the donor, dictates the form this aid is to take.

Some view these programs as legitimate, claiming that the needy have a right to help and that government has an obligation to see that they get it. Others see it differently. They feel that aiding the needy is not a legitimate concern of government and that charitable acts should be made on a strictly voluntary basis. By this reasoning, it is wrong for government to compel us to participate in these programs by financing them through the tax system.

The Total Amount Redistributed.   Some people, after looking at the level of income available to the needy even considering the benefits they receive from these programs, argue that society is not doing enough to redistribute the available wealth. While recognizing the tremendous investment that has been made, these critics argue that the investment is not sufficient, since many American families continue to live in poverty.

Others disagree. While they concur that government should help, they argue that we are spending too much on these programs. These critics look at the tax burden imposed by these programs and conclude that it is too heavy for the average taxpayer to bear. Both sets of critics feel that the current program of redistribution is unfair; the argument is about who is being treated unfairly—the recipients, or the taxpayers?

The Form of Help.   Some redistributive programs give outright cash grants to participants; social security and Aid to Families with Dependent Children are examples. Other redistributive programs give specific goods and services: Medicare and Medicaid provide medical assistance, food stamps indirectly provide food, subsidized housing indirectly provides homes, and so on.

Some people feel that all redistributive programs should provide cash only. This would allow the recipients to spend the money in whatever way they feel is best for them. Those who hold this view claim that the needy should be treated as mature adults with the right to decide for themselves how to use the aid we provide. Other people see it differently. They feel that since the taxpayers are footing the bill, it is the taxpayers who should decide (through their elected representatives) how they want the money spent. This second group feels that it is perfectly legitimate for government to dictate that the aid be in the form of, say, food or medical care or housing, and not in some other form.

The Recipients.   As redistributive programs currently operate, there are very few that provide aid to all and only the needy. The food stamp program is one that attempts to do that: All needy people may receive stamps, and no one may receive stamps unless he is needy. Most redistributive programs, however, are targeted either to aid only some types of needy people or to aid certain groups, not all of whose members are needy. Aid to Families with Dependent Children is a good example of the former type of program. Unless there is a dependent child, a family cannot receive help, no matter how needy it is. Social security is a good example of the latter type of program. All qualified senior citizens are entitled to receive benefits, even though not all who are eligible are in need of help.

Some people claim that we should abolish this system of redistribution of wealth and simply adopt an explicit commitment to come to the aid of all and only those who are needy. Others argue against this proposal on the grounds that only some of the needy are deserving of help. These people would rather retain our current methods of redistribution.

This completes our list of the major value questions that are often raised in connection with the redistribution of wealth through government expenditures. Naturally, both egalitarians and meritocrats have much to say on these issues, and, as we might expect, their views differ considerably. Egalitarians, for the most part, are quite comfortable in defending the legitimacy of these programs, which they see as a system for equalizing the nation's wealth. In fact, they feel we should expand the scope of these programs even further so as to create greater equality in the distribution of wealth among people. Moreover, egalitarians tend to support the idea that we do away with specific types of programs and adopt a general commitment to help all those who are needy.

Meritocrats, for the most part, see things differently. They are troubled because they feel these programs are unfair to those whose hard-earned money is being taken away and given to others who may be less deserving of it. For that reason, many meritocrats oppose the expansion of redistributive programs.

It should be quite clear by now that the topic of the distribution of wealth poses great difficulties for any systematic moral theory. In the next two chapters, we will see how the utilitarian and deontologist approaches attempt to deal with these difficulties.

Exercises

Define in your own words the following terms:

1. egalitarianism
2. meritocracy

3. free market system
4. consumer goods
5. means of production
6. free exchange
7. tax base
8. tax rate
9. distinction between progressive, proportional, and regressive tax rates
10. redistributive program

Review Questions

1. How does egalitarianism and meritocracy challenge the validity of the distribution of wealth in most societies?
2. What are the main components of a free market economy? What impact do these components have upon the distribution of wealth?
3. What are the main choices which are made in setting up any system of taxation?
4. What are the advantages and disadvantages of each of the standard tax bases? Of each of the standard tax rates?
5. In what ways do many nonredistributive government programs contribute to the redistribution of wealth in America?
6. What are the main value questions which must be faced by any redistributive program?

Questions for Further Thought

1. What sorts of arguments, independent of our moral theory, could be offered for egalitarianism and meritocracy?
2. To what extent do we have a free market system in America today? In answering this question, be sure you deal separately with each of the main components of the free market.
3. Could we have a system that combines public ownership of the means of production with free exchanges of goods? Could we have one that combines private ownership of the means of production with very limited freedom in the exchange of goods? Would such mixed systems have any benefits that make them worthy of serious consideration?
4. What explanation would you offer of how America came to have such a hybrid system of taxes? Are there any advantages to such a hybrid system?
5. Consider those government programs which are designed to provide services rather than to redistribute wealth (even if, as we have

seen, they do some of the latter). What would be the advantages and disadvantages of financing such programs by charging fees to those who use the services?

6. This chapter treats social security as a redistributive program rather than as a publicly administered pension program. What are the arguments for and against treating the system this way?

Chapter Seven

The Distribution of Wealth: A Utilitarian Approach

It is evident from the previous chapter that the value questions concerning the distribution of wealth challenge some of the most fundamental institutions in our society. Thus, it is not surprising that there is some disagreement among those who share the utilitarian framework as to what utilitarianism has to say about those questions. This chapter, therefore, presents *a* utilitarian approach to the distribution of wealth; it is not *the only* utilitarian approach to this issue.

7•1 THE BASIS OF OUR UTILITARIAN ANALYSIS

The major premise behind all utilitarian thinking is that the correct solution to any problem is the one that best satisfies human desires. It is not surprising, therefore, that the utilitarian approach to the problem of how wealth should be distributed is to adopt systems which ensure that the wealth will be used most efficiently to satisfy human desires. Let's look at the implications of this idea.

Most utilitarian writers on this topic have adopted the economic principle of *diminishing marginal utility of money*. Simply speaking, what this principle says is that as you increase the amount of wealth you have, each additional dollar you acquire will yield successively smaller contributions to your overall well-being. This seems to make intuitive good sense. When we have only a little bit of money, each additional dollar means quite a lot to us, because it enables us to satisfy some previously frustrated desire. As we acquire more and more wealth, the next dollar begins to mean less and less. Suppose, now, that we have two individuals, one with a great deal of wealth (say, a million dollars) and one with very little wealth (say, $100). Then, the theory of utilitarianism together with the economic principle of diminishing marginal utility of money seem to suggest a powerful argument for taking money from the millionaire and giving it to the person with only $100. The money the millionaire loses represents only a small loss to him compared with the large gain it represents to the poor person, for the former has already satisfied most of his desires while the latter still has many important desires left unsatisfied.

If this analysis were carried to its logical conclusion, it would seem to indicate that society should redistribute wealth until everyone has exactly the same amount. After all, according to the argument we gave above, every time we have one person with more money and another person with less money, we could increase the number and/or importance of desires satisfied by taking money from the one who has more and giving it to the one who has less. However, very few utilitarians have accepted this conclusion. Most argue that there is another important concept to take into account, the *incentive factor*.

Suppose everyone were to receive the same amount of wealth, regardless of how hard they work or how much they contribute to society. Some people, those who work at things they enjoy doing, would presumably labor just as hard and produce just as much as they would otherwise. Most people, however, work at jobs which provide them, at best, with only a modest amount of intrinsic satisfaction. Their major motive for working is to earn money, and their major motive for doing their job well is to receive the rewards that good work earns. If, then, we were to redistribute wealth so that everyone receives the same amount of money, the incentive for working and for working well would disappear for these people. The result would be a tremendous decrease in the amount of wealth produced by society, with a comparable decrease in society's ability to satisfy human desires. Thus, if we want to have the material goods required to satisfy human desires, we need to reward people for their efforts and contributions.

On the one hand, utilitarians recognize the force of the argument for greater equality, and, on the other hand, they support the argument that productivity requires providing incentives through rewards for individual efforts and contributions. As a result, utilitarians find themselves advocating a greater degree of equality than is normally found in societies, while defending a level of inequality sufficient to provide the proper incentives.

By virtue of maintaining this dual position, utilitarians are able to claim that they capture the elements of truth found in both the egalitarian and the meritocratic points of view. Like the egalitarian, the utilitarian advocates increasing the level of equality in our society. Like the meritocrat, he recommends rewarding people for their efforts and contributions. In common with both of them, the utilitarian is opposed to those inequalities of wealth that have nothing to do with rewarding effort and contribution.

Note that this utilitarian analysis pays no attention to such issues as what justice demands by way of distribution of wealth, the rights of people either to have what they need or to keep what they have earned, the fundamental equality of all human beings, and so on. This omission is not surprising. We saw in Chapter 1 that utilitarianism is a monolithic ethical theory, meaning it is concerned solely with maximizing the satisfaction of human desires. For utilitarians, the question is not one of justice or equality or human rights; instead, it is simply how to distribute society's wealth in a way that maximizes the satisfaction of people's desires. Their answer is that we must provide people with the same amount of wealth except for the inequalities that result from incentive rewards for good work and high levels of production. In the rest of this chapter we will see how the utilitarian applies these fundamental ideas to the resolution of the many questions we raised in Chapter 6.

7·2 UTILITARIANISM AND THE FREE MARKET

We saw in section 6.2 that the free market system rests on two major institutions: free exchanges of goods and private ownership of the means of production. In this section we will examine the merits of these two institutions, paying special attention to their implications for the distribution of wealth in society.

In Defense of Free Exchanges of Goods

Utilitarians, for the most part, have advanced a standard argument in defense of free exchanges of goods between people. The argument runs as follows: Suppose person A owns an object, O_1, and person B owns an object, O_2. Suppose, moreover, that A and B agree to exchange their objects. Presumably, they have agreed to this exchange because A thinks he will be better off with O_2 than he is with O_1 and B thinks he will be better off if he has O_1 instead of O_2. In other words, each believes the exchange will lead to a greater satisfaction of his desires. Well, says the utilitarian, this provides us with a justification for allowing this exchange to take place. After all, isn't it reasonable to suppose that A and B are the best judges of what will satisfy their respective desires? If this is so, then the redistribution of goods through free exchange is indeed one which will make both of the parties to the exchange better off—it will lead to greater desire-satisfaction—and so it ought to be allowed.

Let's examine this thesis more carefully. Suppose an unemployed laborer, who has plenty of time but little money, gets together with a factory owner, who has plenty of money but not enough laborers. Suppose, now, that the laborer agrees to work for the employer in return for a certain wage. The employer is happy, because he needs the labor more than he needs the money it will cost him to get it, and the laborer is happy, because he needs the money more than he needs the time and energy it will cost him to earn it. Thus, both parties believe they will be better off as a result of the exchange. And probably they are right in making this judgment, for who knows what is good for them better than they? Therefore, in order to promote the utilitarian goal of maximizing the satisfaction of desires, society should allow this free exchange to take place.

The heart of the utilitarian defense of free exchanges among individuals is very clear: typically they will result in both parties being able to increase the satisfaction of their desires. But there are several important exceptions to this rule—cases in which the utilitarian argument does not work. Two such exceptions are described below.

Imagine a situation in which there is reason to believe that at least one of the parties to an exchange is not the best judge of whether that exchange will benefit him. In such cases, there is no reason to believe that the exchange will increase the extent of desire-satisfaction. The party who is not capable of accurately judging the situation may be agreeing to an exchange that will cause him to lose a great deal. Here we may conclude, on utilitarian grounds, that this exchange should not be allowed. Suppose, for example, that someone is selling products with hidden defects, which the average consumer will not discover until sometime after the purchase. The buyer may believe that he is gaining by purchasing the product, but in fact he is not. Suppose, moreover, that the losses to the buyer outweigh the gains to the seller. In such a case, utilitarians might well conclude that we should not allow the free exchange to take place, even if the consumer wishes to purchase the product. The reason is that the resulting exchange will lead to a net decrease in overall desire-satisfaction.

Now imagine another type of situation, one in which a free exchange between two parties results in losses to a third party, who has not been consulted. Imagine, further, that the losses to the third party outweigh the gains to the two parties who made the agreement. Here, again, the resulting net decrease in overall satisfaction of desires will lead utilitarians to conclude that such an exchange should not be allowed.

In sum, while there are good utilitarian reasons for believing in the free exchange of goods between consenting adults, these reasons do not hold in all cases. Where they cannot be applied, utilitarians must conclude that certain free exchanges between consenting parties should not be allowed. The parties in question may feel that their freedom to act is being unjustly infringed upon, but from the utilitarian point of view, this is irrelevant to the decision. The only criterion is whether the exchange of goods increases or decreases the overall satisfaction of human desires.

In Defense of Private Ownership of the Means of Production

Utilitarians have a general argument designed to show that private ownership of the means of production is a desirable feature of society. Their analysis has two parts.

Step A: The Argument for Ownership.   If we want a great increase in the satisfaction of human desires, we need to see that our natural resources are effectively employed to produce the things that people want. This can only take place if someone owns these resources and transforms them into efficient means of production. To begin with, the effective use of resources as means of production requires a large investment of capital to properly develop them. In exchange for this investment, those who supply the capital must expect to get something in return, otherwise they would have no incentive to invest their money in this way. The more they get in return, the more they will invest. Moreover, when there is ownership of property, particularly ownership which can be passed on in the future, these resources and these means of production are carefully protected from overuse. When you do not have ownership, then people will over use and ruin these items. They have no incentive to protect the future use of the resources since they are not guaranteed that they can use them in the future.

Step B: The Argument for *Private* Ownership. The argument in step A only shows that it is necessary that property be owned; it doesn't specify by whom. In some societies this ownership is in the hands of the state. Such societies have a form of economic organization different from the free market system we are discussing. Utilitarians would claim that state ownership of the means of production is not as effective in properly utilizing society's resources as is a system of private ownership. The private owner, who will reap the benefit of the efficient development and use of the property, has an incentive to see that resources are used to produce what people want and that there is no waste in the process. In systems of state ownership, this type of incentive is not present. The ordinary citizen is too far removed from the decision making to have any impact, while the state managers are concerned with their own interests and have no particular incentive to ensure that the resource is properly used.

You should be aware that this sketch is just the barest outline of the utilitarian argument for private ownership of the means of production. There are many details to fill in, which we cannot do here. We will simply summarize this argument by saying that the utilitarian defense of private ownership of the means of production is based on the idea that only this system can provide the proper incentives to see that society's resources are employed efficiently in the production of the goods required to satisfy human desires. In those cases in which private ownership does not produce these results, utilitarians will not defend private ownership of the means of production.

The major shortcoming of private ownership, as we saw in section 6.1, is that it often leads to significant inequalities in the distribution of wealth. And this, as we pointed out earlier, is not acceptable from the utilitarian point of view. Nevertheless, most utilitarians advocate the system of private ownership of the means of production so as to provide incentives, but they suggest that we use taxes and the redistribution of wealth through government expenditures to even out some of the inequalities it produces.

Let's look at this point from another perspective. We saw in section 7.1 that utilitarians are trying to strike a balance between providing incentives and promoting equality. Their defense of private ownership of the means of production is based on considerations of incentives, so to maintain the balance, they must compensate for the resulting inequalities by urging us to use taxes and government expenditures to redistribute as much wealth as we can without demolishing the incentives.

In short, utilitarians do not take an absolutist position on either the free exchange of goods or the private ownership of the means of production. They believe that, for the most part, each of these aspects of the free market system should be retained subject to:

1. limiting the right of free exchange in those cases in which it will not maximize overall desire-satisfaction.

2. supplementing a system of private ownership of the means of production with a program of taxes and redistribution of wealth substantial enough to even out a good portion of the inequalities produced by private ownership.

7·3 UTILITARIANISM AND TAXATION

As we saw in section 6.1, there are two decisions that every theory of taxation must confront. One is the choice of a tax base and the other is the choice of a rate of taxation. What is the utilitarian approach to each of these decisions?

Most discussions about which tax base to use reflect views as to which base is fairer. Some people consider ability to pay as the foundation of fairness, and they therefore argue for income or wealth as the tax base. Others emphasize that consumption takes from our common resources, and they therefore feel expenditure is the proper basis for taxation. The utilitarian, owing to his monolithic approach, does not look at the choice of a tax base in this way. Instead, he chooses the tax base which will best promote his utilitarian goals.

To see how this works, we need to examine the implications of choosing one or another of the various tax bases. If we choose to tax income, then everybody who receives an income must give up some of what they earn. The more we tax, the less each person gets to keep and the more attractive the alternative of leisure becomes. Thus, a tax on income, at any rate of taxation, is an incentive not to work. And the higher the tax rate, the greater that incentive. Suppose we choose to tax wealth. The same reasoning leads to the conclusion that we are then offering incentives not to accumulate wealth. If we spend our money, we have no wealth on which to pay tax. But if we save it, we are taxed on the wealth we have accumulated. The higher the rate of taxation, the greater the incentive not to save. In short, taxes based on either income or wealth reduce the very incentives that utilitarians strive to promote. Consequently, they suggest that we base our taxes on consumption. Such taxes can be used as the basis for producing the redistribution of wealth that utilitarianism calls for without lessening the incentives that it wishes to maintain.

This idea requires some explanation. Generally, those who are interested in achieving greater equality in the distribution of wealth oppose heavy reliance on consumption taxes. They have in mind the sales tax with which we are all familiar. The reason they oppose such taxes is that they tend to be proportional, and proportional taxes do not go very far toward promoting greater equality in the distribution of wealth. However, the consumption tax which utilitarians favor is not this traditional sales tax. Their basic idea is to devise a method for seeing how much a person has spent each year on the consumption of goods and then use that consumption as a basis for taxation. There is no reason why the resulting consumption tax cannot be as progressive as the utilitarian wants it to be.

This leads us to the second major decision, the choice of a tax rate. As with their analysis of the tax base, utilitarians have their own special approach to deciding on the proper tax rate. It is based on their desire to strike the proper balance between egalitarianism and meritocracy. In order to decrease the inequality in the distribution of wealth, utilitarians advocate progressive tax rates. Their argument runs as follows: by imposing an increasingly higher tax rate as the amount of consumption increases, we take an ever-increasing amount of money from those who have the most wealth. This is certainly a way to cut back on the amount of inequality in society; however, if the tax rate becomes too high, it will begin to lessen people's incentives to work. After all, we work and save with the eventual goal of consuming, and if the tax rate on consumption is too high, then we have less incentive to work and save.

You can see that utilitarians approach the question of taxation from their basic perspective of distributing society's wealth so as to maximize the satisfaction of human desires. They feel that we can only do this by having a greater degree of equality than is normally found in societies while maintaining a sufficient level of inequality to provide the proper incentives. One way to do this is through a progressive rate of taxation on consumption. The progressive feature is to ensure that the tax makes a major contribution toward leveling out inequalities in society, while the use of consumption as the tax base is to help keep down the impact the tax makes on the incentives to work and save.

One final point: In section 6.2 we briefly discussed the inheritance tax, suggesting that it is rather special and controversial. Let's see why. Many people think of the inheritance tax as an ideal tax from the utilitarian point of view. For one thing, since it doesn't tax wealth until the owner of the wealth dies, it would seem to provide little disincentive to work and save. Second, since inherited wealth contributes to the inequality of wealth in society, it would seem that a tax on inheritance would do a good deal toward lessening that inequality. Why, then, does the utilitarian oppose the use of an inheritance tax?

We can answer this question only by understanding that this argument rests on a fundamental confusion. It supposes that inheritance taxes have no impact on people's desires to work and save because it also supposes that people have no interest in what will happen to the money they have earned and saved once they die. Obviously, this cannot be true, for otherwise, people would not make wills, buy life insurance, set up trust funds, and do all the other things they do to ensure that their money is spent the way they want it to be after they die. For such people, leaving money to others is best viewed as a form of consumption, and, presumably, it should be taxed at the same rate. Utilitarians see no reason for taxing inheritances in a special way.

7·4 UTILITARIANISM AND GOVERNMENT REDISTRIBUTIVE PROGRAMS

In section 6.3 we saw that government provides a wide variety of redistributive programs. Some of them are explicitly designed to redistribute wealth from those who have more to those who are needy. Others are not designed for this purpose, but by providing services that are available to everyone, they succeed in redistributing some wealth from those who pay more taxes to those who pay less.

Such redistributive programs give rise to many value questions, such as, Are these programs even legitimate? What amount of redistribution is proper? What are the most appropriate forms of help? and Who are the right recipients? In this final section, we will look at these questions from the utilitarian perspective.

It is clear from what we have seen so far that utilitarians support the legitimacy of massive redistributive programs. They do this not because they believe that the recipients have a right to aid and that the government is obligated to provide that aid. After all, utilitarian theory makes no appeal to rights. For this same reason, they also are not moved by the taxpayers' argument that they have a right to keep the money they make instead of having it taken away in taxes to fund programs they do not want. Utilitarians support government redistributive programs because they believe that the outcome of having these programs—namely, a much greater equality in the distribution of wealth — is desirable because it increases the satisfaction of human desires. In other words, utilitarians accept these programs as legitimate because of the results they produce.

Why can't we simply have programs of private charity which voluntarily redistribute wealth? The utilitarian answer to this question is quite straightforward: Some people will give charity, but many more will not. And of those who do give, they are likely to give much less than the amount that is taken by taxation. Therefore, since utilitarians are looking for a major redistribution of wealth (subject only to the condition that we leave sufficient incentives), they believe that it is best to rely on the government to accomplish this goal, not on private charity.

In the same way that utilitarians have little difficulty justifying the legitimacy of redistributive programs, they also have little difficulty deciding the total amount that should be redistributed. Their view is that we should redistribute enough so as to equalize income except for that amount required to maintain incentives for working and saving. At one time, it was thought that this need not involve a great deal of inequality: that is, an ample incentive required only a modest difference in income. For that reason, utilitarians argued for a near total equalization of wealth through a massive redistributive program. Recent events, however, have cast doubts on this relatively optimistic view of how much equality and how much redistribution is desirable in a utilitarian framework. Such concepts as the Laffer curve and supply-side economics, as well as the economic realities responsible for America's failure to save and produce, have resulted in a growing perception that much more massive incentives are required if we are to have adequate production through work and savings. If these revised views are correct, then the utilitarian approach will have to allow for greater inequalities of income and wealth than were previously acceptable. This will mean a reduction in the amount of redistribution utilitarians can support. Therefore, while utilitarianism has a clear theoretical answer as to how much redistribution should take place in society (namely, as much as possible without doing away with incentives), it is unclear as to exactly how much redistribution we should actually be doing.

As we saw in section 6.3, current programs for redistribution are primarily targeted at various groups, many of whose members are needy, but not directly at the total class of needy people. The view seems to be that there are some needy people who do not deserve help and who therefore should not be helped. This is unacceptable from the utilitarian perspective. The basic idea behind this perspective is that we should redistribute wealth to those who are needy so as to maximize the satisfaction of human desires. Redistributing wealth to some who are not needy (as we do when, for example, we provide social security benefits to wealthy elderly people), or failing to redistribute wealth to those who are needy (as we do when we exclude families without children from some welfare benefits), is not in line with this general goal. Therefore, the utilitarian analysis would support the abolishment of all these special programs and advocate adopting one program that redistributes money to all and only those who need help.

The hardest question from the utilitarian point of view is whether we should simply redistribute money, leaving it for the recipients to spend as they see fit, or distribute in-kind benefits, such as food, low-income housing, medical care, and so on. In general, utilitarians agree with the view that the best judge of what will most satisfy people's desires are the people themselves. Therefore, they are strongly inclined to support redistribution in the form of cash payments. However, even the most ardent supporter of such payments is aware of the exceptional cases in which people are not the best judge of what is best for them. For this reason, some utilitarian analysts are prepared to accept programs of in-kind benefits.

7•5 CONCLUSIONS

In this chapter, we have examined a utilitarian theory of the redistribution of wealth. Its basic idea is that we should adopt systems which will produce as much equality as possible while still maintaining adequate incentives to work and save. As a result, it supports the free market, subject to certain constraints, even though this leads to great inequalities. These inequalities should be lessened through a highly progressive tax on consumption, which would furnish the funds to finance redistributive programs.

All these are highly controversial theses. Here, as elsewhere, utilitarianism is presented as a systematic approach that challenges many commonly accepted institutions. In the next chapter, we shall see what happens to these institutions when they are analyzed from a deontological point of view.

Exercises

Define in your own words the following terms:

1. diminishing marginal utility (of money)
2. incentive factor
3. utilitarian defense of free exchanges

4. efficient use of resources
5. tax on consumption/sales tax distinction
6. in-kind benefits

Review Questions

1. How does the theory of diminishing marginal utility of money serve as the basis for the utilitarian analysis of the distribution of wealth?
2. Why do utilitarians reject a principle of total equality?
3. How does utilitarian theory try to incorporate the insights in both egalitarianism and meritocracy?
4. What are the utilitarian arguments for the free exchange of goods? What limitations would utilitarians put on this freedom?
5. What are the utilitarian arguments for private ownership of the means of production? What limitations would utilitarians put on private ownership?
6. Why would utilitarians probably prefer a progressive tax on consumption?
7. Why would utilitarians oppose a special tax on inheritance?
8. How would utilitarians justify massive redistributive programs? How would utilitarians structure those programs?

Questions for Further Thought

1. Suppose there are some people who continue to get immense desire-satisfaction either from ever further accumulation of money or from what they can buy with their money, no matter how much they have. Would it follow that for these people utilitarians would have a moral obligation to see that they continue to get a great deal of money? Are there, in fact, such people?
2. Could we find incentives other than money that would stimulate hard work and contributions to society so that wealth could be equally distributed? Would this require a different type of person? Could society mold people that way?
3. Would it be possible to develop a system of public ownership of the means of production such that either the ordinary citizen or the state manager would have the incentives to see that resources are properly used to maximize public benefit?
4. Critically evaluate the following utilitarian argument for public ownership of the means of production: "Private ownership may guarantee that resources shall be used to maximize the interest of the owner. But there is no incentive to see that the resources are not used in a way that causes much harm to others. Look, for

example, at all the pollution produced by private industry. Only public ownership can solve this sort of problem."

5. Why will a tax on consumption minimize the disincentive to work and save? After all, people work and save so that they can eventually consume, so a tax on consumption discourages working and saving just as much as does a tax on income or wealth.

6. In light of the strong utilitarian reasons for distributing money rather than in-kind benefits, are there any reasons for supporting such in-kind programs as food stamps and Medicaid?

Chapter Eight

The Distribution of Wealth: A Deontological Approach

By now you undoubtedly expect the familiar disclaimer that the theory we are about to describe is only one version of the application of the deontological approach to the problem under consideration. This chapter contains *a* deontological approach to the value problems concerning the distribution of wealth, not *the only* deontological approach. This warning is particularly important in connection with the distribution of wealth, for different deontologists have arrived at very different conclusions about this problem. In fact, the deontological theory which we present in this chapter is a relatively new one, although it is dependent on early writings in the libertarian tradition.

8·1 THE BASIS OF OUR DEONTOLOGICAL ANALYSIS

Most analyses of the distribution of wealth end with the conclusion that there is some special pattern of wealth distribution required by sound moral principles. For example, the egalitarian concludes that morality requires as much equality as possible in the distribution of wealth. The meritocrat concludes that morality requires that wealth be distributed according to people's efforts and contributions. The utilitarian requires that wealth be distributed in a way which produces as much equality as possible while still maintaining adequate incentives to work and save.

The theory which we will present in this chapter belongs to a minority of theories which does not believe that morality requires a definite pattern for the distribution of wealth. Instead, this theory, and others like it, claims that morality requires only that wealth be obtained by proper processes. These processes may lead to widely different distributions of wealth, and any one of these distributions is acceptable as long as it comes about through a proper process.

A simple example may help illustrate this concept. Jones believes that he and his wife have a right of ownership of the house they live in. Why does he believe this? Because he knows that he and his wife bought that property from someone who had a right to it. The legitimacy of the Joneses' right to that bit of wealth depends on the process through which they acquired that property and not on some predetermined pattern for the proper distribution of wealth.

Let's develop this idea a little more fully. We need to distinguish between two types of legitimate property rights: derivative property rights and original property rights. A *derivative property right* is a property right acquired by legitimate means (e.g., purchase, gift, inheritance) from someone who previously had the rights to that property. An *original property right* is a right acquired in a legitimate fashion on some property which was not previously owned. Thus, our theory can be restated roughly this way: Distribution of wealth is legitimate if it consists of original property rights and/or of derivative property rights.

How does this differ from the utilitarian approach discussed in the last chapter? The utilitarians view property holdings as legitimate if they contribute to the general satisfaction of human desires. To deontologists, property holdings are legitimate because the individuals who own them have a right to them (independent of the general satisfaction of human desires). A legitimate distribution of wealth can take many forms; some will promote the general satisfaction of human desires more than others. But all legitimate distributions are based on original or derivative property rights.

It follows that a theory like ours must depend very heavily on some theory as to how original property rights can be legitimately acquired. Suppose there is some property which is not owned by anyone and which everyone is thus free to use—How can someone acquire, in a legitimate fashion, a right to that property? Drawing upon the ideas of John Locke, these theorists would say that a person may legitimately acquire that original property right by expending his labor so as to increase the value of that piece of property. The basic notion is that we have a right to the increased value which our labor produces; thus, by increasing the value of unowned property, we have a legitimate right to that property.

An example may help bring out this point. Suppose that in the mid-nineteenth century nobody had any special claim to the land on which the Joneses' house now rests. Suppose, further, that someone came along and began to farm an area which includes that land. His labor improved the land, and thereby increased its value. After a few years he built a house there. Through this process he acquired in a legitimate fashion original property rights to the land and house. All subsequent owners, including the Joneses, have held derivative property rights on that land and house, acquired successively by legitimate means, one from another, all the way back to that initial settler.

There is one major difficulty with this account, one that was already noted by contemporaries of John Locke. The objection might be stated like this: Granted that the settler who improved the land has a right to the increased value he produced through his labor, why should it follow that he then has a right to the whole property? After all, since the natural resource had its own initial value, much of the value of the property, and much of his resulting wealth, is independent of his labor. If we allow the settler to own the whole property and not merely the additional value he produced, we are giving him more wealth than he is entitled to. We are allowing him to expropriate the initial value of that resource.

To address this difficulty, we must imagine a group of people meeting to consider the question of how to allow those who labor on unowned natural resources to receive the value produced by their labor, given that such value is mixed up with the initial value of the original resources. One proposed solution to this problem is to negotiate an agreement that: (a) allows the original worker on the property to form property rights over the initial value of the natural resources as well as over the value he has added; (b) compensates those who lose the right to use those natural resources; and (c) offers that compensation in the form of a socially recognized right to a minimum level of support if one becomes indigent.

Think of it this way: The natural resources of the earth are leased to those who develop them, or to those to whom the leases get transferred. In return, the lease holders owe a rental to everyone. That rental is collected as taxes and used to fund a program of redistribution which aids those who are indigent. As with an insurance fund, while all are equally covered, not all receive payouts. In this program, only those who are needy may receive payouts. Since it would be reasonable for such people to agree to such a scheme of original acquisitions of property rights, we may conclude that such a scheme of property rights is legitimate.

In short, this theory says the following: Any distribution of wealth is legitimate providing it consists of legitimately acquired original property rights or legitimately acquired derivative property rights. Original property rights are legitimately acquired if they are based on labor performed on unowned natural resources which improves the value of those resources. An additional condition for legitimacy is that those who acquire the original property rights, or those to whom these rights are transferred, must pay taxes to help finance a scheme of social insurance which redistributes wealth to those who are needy.

8·2 DEONTOLOGY AND THE FREE MARKET

We saw in section 6.1 that one of the crucial components of the free market system is private ownership of the means of production. We also saw there that this private ownership of the means of production plays a prominent role in the accumulation of great wealth. This accumulated wealth can then be passed on through inheritance. As a result, both egalitarians and meritocrats have substantial doubts about private ownership of the means of production.

In Defense of Private Ownership of the Means of Production

All of this looks quite different from the perspective we have been developing in this chapter. Suppose, to take an extreme example, that Smith inherits a great fortune in wealth that has accumulated as a result of his ancestors' ownership of means of production. Is this accumulation of wealth legitimate from the perspective of our deontological theory? If it was accumulated by Smith's ancestors through a legitimate process, and if they truly left this wealth to him, then the answer is yes. This is the whole point of saying that our theory emphasizes the *process* by which wealth is accumulated and not the actual *pattern* of wealth which comes about by this process.

The private ownership of the means of production is perfectly legitimate from the perspective of our theory providing that the people who own these means of production have come to own them either as legitimate original property rights or as legitimate derivative property rights. Egalitarians and meritocrats are troubled about this private ownership of the means of production because they are concerned with its implications for the distribution of wealth. But from the point of view of our deontological theory, these implications are irrelevant. These property holdings will be considered legitimate as long as they were acquired legitimately.

It is important to contrast this defense of private ownership of the means of production with the utilitarian defense. Utilitarians who advocate private ownership do so because they believe that private ownership provides the best incentives for the proper use of our resources. They are troubled, however, about the implications of private ownership for the distribution of wealth, because they are basically in sympathy with egalitarianism. Deontologists justify private ownership of the means of production on the grounds that these means of production rightfully belong to their owners if they were acquired in a legitimate way and as long as the owners pay the proper taxes as compensation. These theorists are less concerned with the implications for the distribution of wealth because they have rejected such patterned approaches as egalitarianism and meritocracy.

In Defense of Free Exchanges of Goods

The deontological argument in defense of the other major component of the free market—free exchanges of goods—proceeds in two steps:

1. Mature adults of sound mind have the right to freely agree with each other to exchange their goods. This right is part of a more general right to do as you choose as long as you do not violate the rights of third parties. Naturally, if one of the parties agrees because he has been forced to do so or because of fraudulent misrepresentation, then we do not have a free exchange, and the state may interfere to protect the party being cheated. In all other cases, it is wrong for the state to interfere with these freely agreed-upon exchanges.

2. When property is freely exchanged, then we have a case of both parties acquiring in a legitimate fashion derivative property rights. Therefore, in such cases, it would be wrong for the state to take from either party the property he has acquired.

Let's see how this can be applied in our labor-contract example. Recall that an employer agrees to transfer some money (wages) to a laborer in return for a given amount of work. Each party has the right to engage in such a transaction, and each has the right to what is transferred to him. It would be wrong for the state to interfere with this freely agreed-upon exchange of goods.

It is instructive to see how the utilitarian defense of the free exchange of goods differs from the deontological defense. Utilitarians defend free exchanges on the grounds that both parties will gain. Deontologists defend free exchanges on the grounds that both parties have the right to engage in such exchanges. The difference becomes crucial in those cases in which one party is making a mistake and will surely stand to lose. Utilitarians, as we saw in section 7.2, are willing to prevent the free exchange of goods in these cases. Deontologists would allow the exchange to go through. They believe that people's right to freely exchange goods includes the right to do so even when everyone else judges that they are making a mistake. But they would have society prevent these exchanges if the potential loser has been forced to consent to the exchange or if his consent was obtained by fraud. Both deontologists and utilitarians also agree that it is correct to block free exchanges when they interfere with the rights of third parties.

In sum, deontologists are strong believers in private ownership of the means of production and in free exchange of goods. These aspects of the free market system are justified providing that: (a) the private ownership comes about by legitimate means and that the requirement to compensate by paying taxes is satisfied; and (b) the exchange of goods is not obtained through force or fraud and it does not violate the rights of others.

Deontologists remain committed to these aspects of the free market system even if the result is a very unequal distribution of wealth. For the deontologist, it is the process by which wealth is acquired that justifies the acquisition, not the pattern of wealth that results. This is not to say that deontologists have no theory of redistribution, for there is the requirement that compensation be paid through taxes. In the next two sections we will see how this requirement operates as the foundation for a theory of redistribution.

8·3 DEONTOLOGY AND TAXATION

As we saw in section 6.2, there are two questions that every theory of taxation must confront. One is the choice of a tax base and the other is the choice of a rate of taxation. Let's examine each of these questions from the deontologists' perspective.

Some would choose income or wealth as a tax base, on the grounds that those with income and/or wealth have the ability to pay. But they have never explained why those who are able to pay should be required to pay, so their argument fails to establish that we should use income or wealth as a tax base. Others would choose consumption as a tax base, because they view consumption as taking from our common resources. However, they never explain why consumption should be viewed this way. After all, it may be argued that the buyer is consuming only what is his, so why should he be taxed on the basis of his consumption? We saw in the last chapter that utilitarians would tax consumption, on the grounds that such a tax best promotes the redistribution of wealth while minimizing the impact on incentives to produce. However, if one rejects the basis of the utilitarian theory of the distribution of wealth, neither of these features justifies the claim that consumption should be taxed.

Deontologists have a different view of the question of the proper tax base. From their perspective, taxation to support redistribution is justified on the basis that it is a way of paying compensation for the original acquisition of property rights over the initial value of the natural resources. We must examine the implications of this viewpoint in order to understand the deontological theory of the proper tax base.

In theory, this approach has no difficulty determining the proper tax base. Holders of original property rights should be taxed on the initial value of the undeveloped land which they have made their own by working on it. Those who subsequently acquire derivative property rights to that land should be taxed on the same base on which the original property holders were taxed. In short, our approach says that the proper tax base is the initial value of originally acquired property rights.

Let's put this point another way. When people acquire original property rights, they simultaneously acquire certain obligations to pay taxes. The amount of their obligation is based on the initial value of the undeveloped property; that is, its value before any labor was performed on it. Thus, we may think of these bits of property as coming with a certain tax liability. As the holders of these original rights transfer their property to other people, those people also acquire the tax liability. In this way, at least in theory, we know what the basis of taxation ought to be.

The same considerations suggest what the rate of taxation ought to be. It ought to be proportional to the initial value of the originally acquired property. The intuitive idea is this: For each unit of initial value you acquire through original property rights, you owe a unit of taxes to help society compensate those who are needy. This theory gives rise to a proportional tax.

Although this scheme is easy to state in principle, it is extremely difficult to apply in practice, for over the centuries, we have lost track of who owes what taxes. What we need to do is find a tax base and a tax rate which will reasonably approximate what should in theory be the proper taxes. It has been suggested that a proportional tax on wealth is the best approximation. Taxes on consumption are totally unrelated to our theoretical ideal. A wealthy miser would be taxed very little by a consumption tax, but he would owe a great deal if he were taxed on the basis of his property and its accompanying obligations. And the more extensive his property, the more substantial his tax bill. Similarly, a foolish investor, who earns very little income on his substantial wealth, would be taxed very little by a tax based on income. But a tax based on wealth would give him a substantial tax bill. These sorts of considerations suggest that the best we can do in the real world to approximate our ideal scheme is to tax people proportionally to their wealth.

It is interesting to note that neither the utilitarian analysis (offered in section 7.3) nor the deontological analysis of this section lends any support to the current practice of progressive income taxes. The reader might well want to consider whether there is any moral basis for defending our current tax scheme.

It is also interesting to note certain practical differences between this proportional tax on wealth and the progressive tax on consumption advocated by the utilitarian approach. Particularly if the rate of progression advocated by the utilitarian is quite high, the utilitarian system of taxes is likely to lead to a greater redistribution of wealth than is our proportional tax on wealth. This is not surprising. The utilitarian analysis begins with a stronger positive feeling in favor of equalizing wealth. In fact, the only reason for stopping short of complete equalization is because of the need to preserve incentives. Since the deontological approach begins with no such feeling in favor of equalization, it winds up with less redistribution. Second, the utilitarian approach offers people a substantial incentive for avoiding consumption. The more you consume, the more you will be taxed. This bias against consumption seems to accept indirectly the idea (offered by other advocates of taxes on consumption) that the consumer is taking away what belongs to society in general and must pay a tax for doing so. The deontological approach, which sees the individual property holder as really owning his property if he acquires it legitimately, views consumption differently. If the wealth really is yours, then you have a perfect right to consume it — if that is what you want — and society has no right to discourage that consumption through taxation. As long as you pay the taxes you owe on your wealth, society should be neutral about the way in which you use the rest of it.

To summarize, our deontological theory suggests that the proper way to fund government programs of redistribution is through a proportional tax on wealth. Such a tax seems to be the best approximation of an ideal tax in which each taxpayer would pay his appropriate share based on the initial value of all originally acquired property rights which have been transferred to him.

8·4 DEONTOLOGY AND GOVERNMENT REDISTRIBUTIVE PROGRAMS

We saw in section 6.3 that government is engaged in a wide variety of redistributive programs. Some of them are explicitly designed to redistribute wealth from those who have more to those who are needy. Others are not designed for this purpose. However, because they provide government services, whether or not the recipients pay for them in the form of taxes, they actually succeed in redistributing some wealth.

Such redistributive programs give rise to many value questions. These include the question of the very legitimacy of these programs, of the proper total amount to be redistributed, of the proper forms of help, and of the proper recipients. In this section, we look at these questions from the deontological perspective.

It is clear from what we have seen so far that deontologists support the legitimacy of at least some redistributive programs. They do this because they believe that the recipients have a right to such aid and that the government is the proper institution to provide it. After all, one of the conditions for justifying the acquisition of original property rights is that those who acquire them, and those to whom these rights are subsequently transferred, must pay taxes to help finance a scheme of social insurance which redistributes wealth to those who are needy. The needy have the right to those payments as compensation for having lost the right to use the natural resources which are now owned by others. By the same reasoning, deontologists are not moved by the taxpayer argument that he has a right to keep the money being taken from him in taxes. After all, the taxpayer also has an obligation to pay the taxes which support the program of redistribution, for without the appropriate compensation payments, his property rights become invalid. In short, it follows from our theory that property holders have an obligation to pay certain taxes to fund redistributive programs and that the indigent have a right to receive certain payments from that program.

Why don't we simply have programs of private charity, which voluntarily redistribute wealth? The deontological response to this proposal is quite straightforward: Payments to finance a redistributive program are not a question of charity; they are obligations which fall upon those who own property. Therefore, any reliance on voluntary donations would enable some people to avoid their obligations.

The next value question that arises in connection with these redistributive programs is that of the proper total amount to be redistributed. In other words, How much should we take by taxation from the property holders to redistribute to the needy? Some would answer this solely in terms of the needs of the indigent: they would say that the proper amount is that which can satisfy all the legitimate needs of those who require help. The deontologist, however, rejects that answer because it fails to consider the total amount owed by the property holders. Suppose, for instance, that there are many who are indigent and that satisfaction of their needs would require an amount greatly in excess of the obligations of property holders. If we were to tax enough to meet all their needs, we might have to tax away a very large proportion of the property held by taxpayers. There is nothing in our theory which would justify such a high level of taxation.

The deontologist approaches the question from the perspective of property holders' obligations rather than from the perspective of indigents' needs. Therefore, society should, to the extent possible, impose a tax equal to what would be a fair rental value on the initial, undeveloped, originally acquired natural resources. Of course, it would be very difficult to calculate exactly how much that might come to, but it seems unlikely that it could amount to more than a modest percentage of society's total wealth. This sum of money would be available for redistribution, and it should be redistributed to the poor in proportion to their need. The actual level of benefits received by the needy would be determined by the total number of dollars legitimately raised by taxes divided by the total number of recipients. The amount of help will vary in proportion to changes in this ratio.

To exemplify how this might work, suppose that the total wealth of society is $1,000 and that the needs of the indigent could be satisfied by $500. If we tax the property holders the full amount required to meet the needs of the indigent, we would have to tax their wealth at a 50 percent tax rate. From our present perspective, it is highly unlikely that this would be a fair tax burden. If, as seems more likely, a fair tax rate would be, say, 10 percent of the total wealth, then $100 would be raised from taxation, and each indigent person would meet 20 percent of his needs from the government redistributive program. Naturally, if the amount of wealth in society increases, say to $5,000, while the needs of the indigent do not increase, then our system of taxation would raise $500, and we could meet all the needs of the indigent.

As we saw in section 6.3, current programs of redistribution are primarily targeted at specific groups, many of whose members are needy; however, they are not targeted directly at the total class of needy people. The assumption seems to be that there are some needy people who do not deserve the help and who should not be helped. Deontologists disagree. From their perspective, we should redistribute wealth to those who are needy so as to compensate them for the loss of the right to use the earth's privately owned natural resources. Redistributing wealth to some who are not needy (as we do when we provide social security benefits to wealthy elderly people) or failing to redistribute wealth to those who are needy (as we do when we exclude people without children from certain types of welfare benefits) is not in line with this obligation. Therefore, our deontological analysis would agree with the utilitarian analysis in supporting the abolishment of all these special programs and the adoption of one program for redistributing money to all the indigent, regardless of their individual circumstances.

Shall we distribute cash money, leaving it for the recipients to spend as they see fit? Or, shall we distribute in-kind benefits, such as food, low-income housing, medical care, and so on? The deontological analysis seems to support the former method. The money distributed to the needy is, after all, something they have a right to by way of compensation. If it is theirs, it would seem that they should be free to spend it as they please rather than receive it in forms that dictate its use.

8·5 CONCLUSIONS

In this chapter, we have examined a deontological theory of the redistribution of wealth. Its basic idea is that any distribution of wealth is legitimate providing that (a) it consists of legitimately acquired original property rights or legitimately acquired derivative property rights and (b) it is accompanied by a proportional tax on wealth. This approach supports the free market system, even if it leads to vast inequalities of wealth. These inequalities should be lessened through a redistributive program, funded by the taxes collected, which compensates the needy for the private expropriation of the earth's natural resources.

These are all highly controversial theses, and they are in strong contrast with some conclusions of the utilitiarian analysis. Neither analysis, however, supports current practice in this area. The reader might well wonder whether there is any analysis that would support our current practice. If, however, we are to give up current practice, we will need to resolve the fundamental dispute between utilitarianism and deontology, for they do lead to very different new approaches to the distribution of wealth in society.

Exercises

Define in your own words the following terms:

1. patterned theories of distributive justice

2. derivative property rights/original property rights distinction
3. labor theory of original property rights
4. social insurance scheme
5. ability to pay theory of taxation
6. taxes as compensation
7. right to welfare

Review Questions

1. In what sense is the theory developed in this chapter a nonpatterned theory of distributive justice (that is, one that does not believe in a definite pattern for the distribution of wealth)?
2. What is the Lockean theory of original property rights? What are its strengths and weaknesses?
3. In what way does the theory developed in this chapter show that property rights require redistribution of wealth to ensure their legitimacy?
4. How does the deontological justification of private property differ from the utilitarian justification? What are their respective strengths and weaknesses?
5. How does the deontologist justify free exchanges of goods?
6. Why does the deontological theory of justice lead to the conclusion that an ideal scheme for taxation is one based on original obligations acquired with original property rights? Why does it lead to the conclusion that, in practice, we should have a proportional tax on wealth?
7. Why do deontologists support redistributive programs as opposed to voluntary charity?
8. How would deontologists structure redistributive programs?

Questions for Further Thought

1. If a person can acquire initial property rights through his labor, why doesn't every worker whose labor improves the value of some property own that property? Why does the property continue to be owned by his employer?
2. Suppose that we could show that everyone, even the poorest, is better off under a system that supports ownership of private property than in a world without private property rights. Then would it still be necessary to compensate the indigent through welfare programs?
3. How does the deontological defense of the free exchange of goods, as offered in this chapter, compare to its critique of victimless crimes offered in Chapter 5?

4. Many Marxists criticize the labor contract on the grounds that it is not really a free exchange of goods. They claim that the worker is coerced by his poverty into accepting terms that are unfair. Is that a legitimate critique of the free exchange model of the labor contract?

5. We have found in the text little support for the idea of a progressive income tax. Are there any arguments, either utilitarian or deontological, for that familiar scheme?

6. Why is it likely that utilitarianism would support a higher level of redistribution than would the deontological scheme? Can that fact, if it is a fact, provide a basis for preferring one approach to the other?

Chapter Nine

Value Problems Concerning Life and Death

9·1 INTRODUCTION

Our major emphasis so far in this book has been on value problems arising out of our fundamental legal and social institutions. Here and in the next two chapters we shift our focus and concentrate on a set of value problems arising out of personal and individual decisions about life and death. This is not to say that these problems lack a social and/or legal dimension. In fact, they are very much a matter of social and legal concern. We simply wish to focus on them from the perspective of choices made by individuals, not from the point of view of their implications for legal rules and social institutions.

The three main problems with which we shall be concerned are suicide and euthanasia, abortion, and the allocation of scarce medical resources. All these issues have been extensively discussed both in scholarly publications and in the popular press. And all tend to excite considerable controversy, because people's attitudes toward these problems are quite often widely divergent and strongly held. Our purpose is not to advocate one view over another. Instead, we will follow our usual pattern, first examining some of the main problems and controversies surrounding these issues and then looking at them both from the utilitarian and the deontological perspectives.

Although these problems are not new, there is no doubt that they have become more pressing in recent years. It is worth noting some of the factors responsible for this increasing urgency.

Advances in Medical Technology. One of the effects of modern medicine is that people now live longer than they used to. Moreover, we are now able to sustain life artificially, via machines that can take over vital functions that the body can no longer perform. While the benefits of this technology are incalculable, it has also forced us to rethink our attitudes about suicide and euthanasia. We must now answer questions, such as — When does life end? Might one prefer death to a life that is dependent on a machine? — that could not even have been asked before. Medical technology has also raised new questions about abortion. If we know for a fact that a child will be born with a severe mental and/or physical handicap (as we are now able to know in certain cases), is an abortion more justifiable? Furthermore, abortion is now at least as safe for the mother as pregnancy. Statistics show that in many countries today, the mortality rate for women who have abortions in the first three months of pregnancy is lower than the mortality rate for women who bear a child. Thus, many women who once might not have considered an abortion for fear of medical complications are now quite willing to consider it. In these respects, advances in medicine have increased the demand for abortions. Finally, advances in medical technology have produced some extremely complicated and expensive forms of life-saving treatment. Transplant oper-ations are good examples. Only some can be saved and then only at great expense. These advances in medical technology present new problems concerning the allocation of scarce life-saving resources.

Changes in Social Circumstances.   Another factor that has made many of these problems more pressing is the series of social changes that has occurred within a relatively brief period of time. In contem-porary American society, few of us live in an extended family, in which several generations live together in close proximity. As a result, a great many of our old people live as cast-offs, lonely and forgotten. In earlier times, however, the elderly lived with considerable honor and respect among their entire extended family. Not surprisingly, this modification in social customs has had a great impact upon our attitudes toward suicide and euthanasia. Moreover, the recent changes in career pat-terns for women have produced changes in our thinking about abor-tion. As women become increasingly more viable in the marketplace, they attach more and more importance to family planning. Naturally, contraception remains the first line of defense against unwanted preg-nancy. However, since we have not yet devised an ideal method of contraception, there are still a considerable number of unwanted pregnancies, and these women will turn to abortion as a last-resort method of family planning. These are only two examples of the many ways in which our sense of urgency concerning life and death value problems has increased because of recent changes in social cir-cumstances.

Shifting Moral Values.   At an earlier period in history, many of the questions that concern us here seemed to be adequately dealt with by relatively straightforward moral rules. For instance, the notion of the sanctity of human life and the prohibition against killing seemed, at least to many, to settle any questions about suicide, euthanasia, and abortion: they were simply prohibited. Similarly, these same rules seemed to dictate that we spend whatever was required to adequately eliminate the problem of how to allocate scarce medical resources. These types of clear-cut moral resolutions seem less available to us today. Our vastly increased store of information has brought com-plexity to these once rather simple moral issues. As a result, we find them much more difficult to resolve than our ancestors did.

In short, then, advances in medical technology, changes in social circumstances, and shifts in moral conceptions have led to a great sense of uncertainty about some extremely important issues of life and death. Therefore, we need to examine each of these value problems carefully, first on its own and then in light of the conflicting ap-proaches of utilitarianism and deontology.

9·2 SUICIDE AND EUTHANASIA

In this section we look at a number of the popular arguments for and against the *moral* permissibility of suicide and euthanasia. We will not be concerned with the legal and societal implications of these acts. To begin with, we need a clear definition of suicide and euthanasia. Suicide is self-inflicted death. Euthanasia is often thought of as mercy killing; it may be voluntary or involuntary, but each is distinguished from murder. In *voluntary euthanasia*, the person who is killed has requested that someone kill him. It is this request that distinguishes voluntary euthanasia from murder. In *involuntary euthanasia*, the person who is killed has not requested that someone kill him, but he is killed for his own benefit, to end his suffering. In many such cases, the victim is incapable of making such a request, because he has lost his capacity to think and/or to express his thoughts. What distinguishes involuntary euthanasia from murder is the benevolent intention on the part of the person who commits the act.

With these definitions clearly in mind, let us now turn to the question of suicide. The first thing to note is that some suicides are *heroic*; that is, acts which nearly everyone would heartily praise as noble and courageous. Consider, for example, a test pilot who chooses not to bail out of his disabled plane in order to stay with it to guide it to crash in an area where no one on the ground will get hurt. Faced with a choice between his life and the lives of many others, he chooses to die. Yet, while this is technically an act of suicide, few—even among those who normally oppose suicide—would condemn the pilot's decision. Suicidal acts of self-sacrifice to save the lives of many others is not what the moral controversy of suicide is all about.

The controversy over the moral permissibility of suicide centers around a different type of case. We are talking here about a person who is contemplating taking his own life because he believes he would be better off dead than alive. Perhaps he is terminally ill and does not want to go through the agony of a slow death. Perhaps he has suffered a great loss, such as the death of his wife, and feels that life is no longer worth living. Those who believe that suicide is morally permissible claim that there is nothing morally objectionable to the person taking his own life when he forms such a judgment. Naturally, to say that suicide is morally permissible is not to say that all who choose to commit suicide do so wisely. Unfortunately, in the stress and strain of life, many who choose to end their own lives do so for tragically mistaken reasons. All that is claimed by those who hold the permissive view about suicide is that the person who commits suicide has done no moral wrong.

Those who object to suicide on moral grounds offer a wide variety of arguments. They claim that suicide is morally impermissible because it is an offense against other people or against the state or against God, or all of these. Let's look at each of these objections more carefully.

Offenses Against Other People.   All of us have a wide variety of obligations that we have incurred over the years. We have obligations to support and comfort members of our families. We have obligations to aid our friends. We have obligations to fulfill various promises we have made. When someone commits suicide, he typically leaves at least some of these obligations unfulfilled. The person who commits suicide has acted wrongly, therefore, precisely because he has acted in a way that makes it impossible for him to fulfill his obligations to other people.

Offenses Against the State.   Everyone who lives in an organized society, it is often argued, has an obligation to further the well-being of that society. No person who has lived for many years in a society has not benefited in many ways from the existence of that society, and therefore no one can say that he does not owe society a debt. We fulfill that debt by being active and productive citizens, doing the best we can to further the well-being of our society. Since the person who commits suicide prevents himself from fulfilling this obligation, his act is therefore morally wrong.

Offenses Against God.   God, it is often claimed, is the source of all life. Because He gave us life, He in some ways owns our life. It is His decision as to how long we shall live and how we shall die. The person who commits suicide acts wrongly against God—in part because he has preempted that role of ruler over life and death, which properly belongs only to God, and in part because, since his life belongs to God, he has no right to dispose of it.

To summarize, those who advocate the moral permissibility of suicide do so primarily on the grounds that the person who commits suicide has a right to do so. It is his life to use or to dispose of as he sees fit. Those who claim that suicide is morally impermissible argue, to the contrary, that the person who commits suicide is thereby failing to fulfill some of his obligations to other people, to society, or to God, and he is acting wrongly precisely because he is failing to fulfill those obligations.

It follows logically that those who consider suicide morally impermissible will also see euthanasia, whether voluntary or involuntary, as impermissible. After all, the distinguishing feature of voluntary euthanasia is that the killing is requested by the person who dies. If, however, it would be wrong for that person to take his own life, then the fact that he has requested that someone else take his life is certainly not going to justify that killing. Similarly, in the case of involuntary euthanasia, if it would be wrong for *you* to take your own life because you judge yourself better off dead, it certainly cannot be right for someone else to take your life because *he* judges that you would be better off dead.

The issue is more complicated when we examine the question of euthanasia from the perspective of those who find suicide morally permissible. Many have gone on to conclude that at least voluntary euthanasia must also be morally permissible. After all, if it is morally permissible for someone to take his own life, why shouldn't he be allowed to ask someone else to do it for him, and why shouldn't that person be allowed to respond to his request? Involuntary euthanasia is a far more troublesome issue. After all, the victim has not requested that he die, and it is precisely for this reason that some who approve of suicide and of voluntary euthanasia object to involuntary euthanasia. Others, however, accept involuntary euthanasia. They reason that since the moral permissibility of suicide and voluntary euthanasia lies in the belief that the victim is better off dead, then the same belief must support the moral permissibility of involuntary euthanasia.

We can summarize the issue of suicide and euthanasia by classifying three major camps:

1. those who believe that neither suicide nor any form of euthanasia is morally permissible
2. those who believe that suicide and voluntary euthanasia are morally permissible but see involuntary euthanasia as morally impermissible
3. those who have no moral objection to suicide or to either form of euthanasia

One final point should be noted in regard to these issues. Many people distinguish *active* from *passive suicide* and *active* from *passive euthanasia*. What this means is that they object to an intentional act of killing, either of oneself or of someone else (even if the other person requests his death and/or would benefit from his death), but they do not object to a *failure to act* in a way that would save one's own life or the life of someone else. This view raises some important questions, such as, Can we really distinguish these cases? and, If we can, does the distinction have any moral significance? We will examine these questions, as well as the other positions we have discussed, in the next two chapters.

9·3 ABORTION

One of the most controversial and widely discussed moral issues of recent years is that of abortion. This issue is so important to people that it played a large role in the 1980 presidential and congressional elections, in which antiabortion groups worked hard to defeat candidates they perceived as being proabortion. Ever since the Supreme Court decision of 1973, which legalized abortion, many groups have been working for a constitutional amendment to overthrow the decision while others have been just as diligent in their efforts to uphold the Court's decision. Most of these public disputes are over the question of whether abortion should be legal. This is not our concern here. We are simply addressing the moral permissibility of abortions. It is important that you keep this distinction in mind as we examine the various positions and arguments pertaining to this topic.

There are three major positions on the question of abortion. The most permissive claims that abortion is always morally permissible, even though it might be imprudent or insensitive in some cases. The least permissive position claims that abortion is never morally permissible (except perhaps in cases of an immediate threat to the woman's life). In between these extremes lies the view that abortions are sometimes morally permissible. For example, abortion is permissible in cases where the health and/or life of the woman is seriously threatened, where the fetus is likely to be seriously deformed, where the fetus is a product of rape or incest, and so forth. In the balance of this section we will examine each of these positions in turn.

There are two standard arguments in support of the most permissive position. The first is based on the claim that fetuses do not have the rights guaranteed to ordinary citizens, such as the right to life or to bodily integrity. Furthermore, among the rights of ordinary citizens is the right of women to be able to control what happens to and in their own bodies, as well as the right to decide when and whether to become a mother. Given these rights, and the lack of any protective rights for the fetus, it is easy for defenders of this position to conclude that it should always be permissible for a woman to have an abortion if that is what she wants. While they recognize that abortion may sometimes be imprudent for health reasons, or that it may be insensitive to the sanctity of life, these people argue that the woman's right to decide her own fate makes the abortion permissible. The second argument in support of this most permissive position claims that while the fetus has some rights, the woman's rights overrule those of the fetus.

The opposite, least permissive, position takes an entirely different tack. Its fundamental assumption is that the fetus—either from the moment of conception or, in any case, from an early stage of development—has the same right not to be killed that is possessed by any other human being. This fetal right to life, like the right to life of other human beings, is fundamental and, as such, takes precedence over most other rights. In particular, it takes precedence over the woman's right to control her body. Consequently, argue supporters of this position, abortion is almost always wrong. There is disagreement, however, as to whether an abortion is morally permissible in cases where the life of the woman is in jeopardy. Some claim that it is, comparing such an abortion to killing someone in self-defense. In other words, even if the fetus has the same full right to life as other human beings, the woman, as an act of self-defense, is morally justified in choosing to have an abortion. Those who would deny the woman's right to an abortion even when her life is threatened claim that the analogy to self-defense is inappropriate. The fetus, they say, is an innocent bystander, not a potential murderer, and the woman has no right to destroy it in order to save her own life.

The intermediate position on the permissibility of abortions tends to utilize parts of each extreme position. Some who take this moderately permissive stance argue that fetuses do have the right not to be killed but that this right is weaker for fetuses than for other human beings. Therefore, in cases of substantial need, the fetus's right to life is outweighed by other factors, and the abortion is permissible. Other defenders of this intermediary position reject the view that the fetus has a right to life but believe that abortions without serious need are nevertheless morally impermissible on the grounds that they reflect insufficient respect and reverence for human life.

In setting out these positions, and the arguments for them, we have not mentioned many of the most familiar pro- and antiabortion arguments. For example, there is the argument for retaining legalized abortions on the grounds that otherwise women will get them illegally, and dangerously. On the other side of the issue, there is the argument that it is wrong to legalize abortions because once we do we are taking a step down the path toward legalizing many other forms of killing. We have deliberately avoided these and other familiar arguments because they are addressed to the question of whether abortion should be legalized. And as we stressed above, our concern here is only with the question of whether abortion is morally legitimate.

As we look back over the positions and arguments concerning the moral legitimacy of abortion, two issues emerge as being centrally important:

1. The status of the fetus: Is the fetus a human being with a right to life? If not, why not? If so, is its right to life as compelling as the right to life enjoyed by people already born?

2. Implications concerning the fetus's status: If the fetus is a human being with a strong right to life, are abortions ever morally permissible? If the fetus is not a human being, under what circumstances are abortions morally wrong?

We will return to these two fundamental issues when we examine the question of abortion from the deontological and utilitarian perspectives. For now, at least, it is clear that the bulk of the discussions about abortion centers around these themes.

9·4 ALLOCATION OF SCARCE MEDICAL RESOURCES

In recent years miraculous developments have taken place in the field of medical science. Chief among these has been the discovery of techniques which offer the prospect of life to people who otherwise would die. Unfortunately, these techniques are often initially available only to a very few people. Usually, it takes several years before they become sufficiently well known, or before the equipment is widely available, or before the costs are within an affordable range. In the meantime, those who have developed the techniques are forced to choose whom to save and whom to let die. This agonizing choice raises some of the most fundamental value issues about life and death.

An analogy is often drawn between these cases and the problem of deciding whom to save among the wounded on a battlefield. Out of the extraordinary circumstances of war, where medical facilties may suddently be swamped by the arrival of large numbers of wounded soldiers, a system was developed for dividing the wounded into three groups. Those who will probably live without help are put aside to be helped later; those whose chances of surviving are minimal, even with help, are simply allowed to die; and those who have a good chance of surviving if they are treated but who will probably die otherwise are the first to receive medical attention. The basic idea behind this system of division is quite simple. On a battlefield, medical resources are extremely scarce. They are best used in the way that maximizes the number of lives they can save. In an analogous fashion, new life-saving techniques are also scarce medical resources, and those who provide them should offer them first to whomever has the best chance to survive with the help of the technique but would surely die without it.

This analogy, which has been widely accepted, certainly focuses our attention on which group of potential recipients should be chosen. It tells us that scarce medical resources should be given first to those whose chance of surviving with them is very high but whose chance of surviving without them is very low. The basic moral principle, that we should use our scarce medical resources to maximize the number of lives saved, seems appropriate. However, this analogy does not totally resolve our problem. There may be far more people who fall into the category of appropriate recipients than can be treated by the scarce medical resources available. The problem remains as to how we should choose from among this group.

An example may help bring out this point. In the first stages of the development of kidney dialysis, only a very limited number of people could be treated. Yet there were a great many people who fitted the medical criterion of being likely to survive if treated but likely to die otherwise. So physicians had the terrible choice of whom to save and whom to let die. While this problem no longer applies to kidney dialysis, it continues to remain today as other life-saving techniques are developed.

A number of approaches have been suggested, including those discussed below.

First Come, First Served.   The basic idea here is that each person who meets the medical criteria has a right to the resource, and the first eligible person to arrive requesting the resource should receive it. The second who arrives should also receive it, and so on until the resource is no longer available. At that point, having no option, the providers of the resource must turn away all additional eligible people who show up. But until that point, it is wrong for them to turn away any eligible person who comes, since all who meet the criteria have a right to be saved.

Random Choice.   As with the last approach, this one also says that everyone who needs the resource and who meets the medical criteria has a right to be treated, and each person has the same right. Unfortunately, we cannot treat everyone. And this approach suggests that the only fair way of dealing with the problem is to provide each eligible person with an equal chance to receive the treatment. A random selection, such as a lottery, is the only way of giving everyone an equal chance to be saved. Any other procedure violates this demand of equality.

Weighing the Lives in Question.   This approach holds that while all who meet the medical criteria are equally in need and equally likely to benefit, there are other factors that differentiate them from one another. For example, some of those in need of the scarce medical resource make important contributions to society, and the failure to save them would be a great loss. Surely we must weigh that fact in deciding whom to save. Some people have families that depend upon them, while others do not. Surely that fact must also be weighed. Some are young, with the possibility of a whole lifetime before them; others are much older, they have already lived most of their lives. Surely this, too, must be considered. In short, this third approach suggests that we should decide whom to save by weighing the gains from saving some against the loses of letting others die. We then must choose to save those whose lives hold the greatest promise of gain.

The great moral difficulty in this area is that all these arguments seem quite plausible. Unfortunately, they cannot all be right. But which is right and which wrong remains unclear. Fortunately, our two systematic moral approaches can provide us some assistance in clearing things up.

Exercises

Define in your own words the following terms:

1. suicide
2. heroic suicide
3. voluntary euthanasia
4. involuntary euthanasia
5. active/passive distinction for suicide and euthanasia
6. least permissive position on abortion
7. most permissive position on abortion
8. moderately permissive position on abortion
9. first come, first served approach to the allocation of scarce medical resources
10. random-choice approach
11. weighing-the-lives approach

Review Questions

1. What are the major factors which have made these life and death questions seem more pressing?
2. What are the major arguments normally offered for and against the moral permissibility of suicide?
3. How are views of the moral permissibility of suicide related to views on the moral permissibility of euthanasia?
4. What are the major arguments for and against the most permissive position on abortion? For and against the least permissive position? For and against the intermediate position?
5. What are the major approaches which have been adopted for allocating scarce medical resources? What are the strengths and weaknesses of each of them?

Questions for Further Thought

1. There are people who claim that suicide is always wrong. Is there any way for them to approve of those cases which we have called heroic suicide?
2. The case of Karen Quinlan seems to be a case of involuntary euthanasia, since she was incapable of consenting because of her condition. On the other hand, much testimony was offered as to her views on the topic, suggesting that she would have consented if she could have. Is there then a special category between voluntary and involuntary euthanasia? If so, how should it be treated?

3. What are the various plausible positions as to when a fetus becomes a human being with a right to life? What are the strengths and weaknesses of each of these?

4. We have focused on the question of the moral permissibility of abortion rather than on the question of what the law should say about abortion. What is the relation, if any, between these two questions?

5. This chapter has assumed that in the allocation of scarce medical resources, the goal is to maximize the *number* of lives saved. Critically evaluate the suggestion that we would do better to focus on the *quality* of the lives saved.

6. Critically evaluate the following objection to both the random choice and the first come, first served approaches: "Both these approaches should be rejected because they rest important decisions on such irrelevant facts as who comes first and who is chosen in the random process."

Chapter Ten

Questions of Life and Death: A Utilitarian Approach

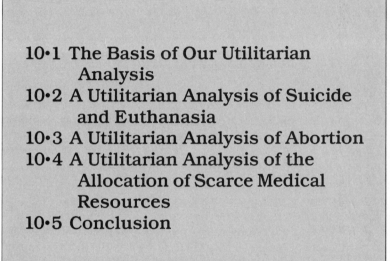

We have seen in earlier chapters how utilitarianism can lead to conclusions that are at striking variance with our normal moral beliefs. Utilitarians point to this variance as evidence that our ordinary beliefs suffer because they are not based on a systematic moral theory. But critics of utilitarianism use this to support their argument that utilitarianism should be rejected because it conflicts with our intuitive sense of truth about morality.

The contrast between the conclusions of utilitarianism and our ordinary moral beliefs is especially pronounced in the area of life and death decisions. We will see shortly how the utilitarian theory seems to lead to some radically new conclusions. It is, therefore, extremely important to keep in mind that not all utilitarians would agree with all the conclusions we will draw; our analysis is *a* utilitarian approach to these problems, it is not *the only* utilitarian approach.

10·1 THE BASIS OF OUR UTILITARIAN ANALYSIS

The main thing to keep in mind is that utilitarians reject the view that taking the life of a human being is intrinsically wrong and that saving the life of a human being is intrinsically desirable. They reject this view not because they approve of killings and disapprove of saving lives but because, in general, they reject the view that *anything* is either intrinsically right or intrinsically wrong. Utilitarianism is, after all, a consequentialist form of moral reasoning. Thus, for utilitarians, killing is wrong only when it leads to bad consequences. Saving lives is right only when it leads to good consequences.

What are some bad consequences of taking the life of a human being? Since the dead person clearly is not suffering any pain, the hedonistic version of utilitarianism—which claims that the only thing that makes consequences bad is pain, and the only thing that makes consequences good is pleasure—has a lot of difficulty answering this question. It is this sort of difficulty that supports our decision in Chapter 1 to reject the hedonistic version of utilitarianism. We replaced hedonism with the view that consequences are good when they result in the satisfaction of desires and bad when they result in the frustration of desires. This version of utilitarianism is in a much better position to answer our question. According to it, the bad consequences of taking a human life are the frustrated desires of the person who is killed and of others. Which desires? To begin with, it frustrates someone's undoubtedly very intense desire to continue living. Moreover, that person is likely to have a wide variety of other desires (goals to accomplish, experiences to have, etc.) which will not be satisfied if he is killed. Finally, killing the person will frustrate the desires of all those who cannot continue to engage in various relations with him.

In short, under normal circumstances, it is wrong to take the life of a human being because such an act will frustrate a great many desires. Similarly, it is ordinarily right to save the life of a human being because that act will lead to the satisfaction of many desires (such as, the individual's desire to continue living, his many other desires which presuppose that he continue living, the desires of others to continue to have relations with him, etc.). Our version of utilitarianism, therefore, has no difficulty explaining why killing is normally very wrong, and why saving human lives is normally the right thing to do.

This way of thinking does, however, have many important corollaries which carry significant implications for our problems of suicide, euthanasia, abortion, and the allocation of scarce medical resources. We will outline some of the major theoretical corollaries just below, and then discuss their implications in the following sections of this chapter.

The Person's Desires Are Very Important.   Suppose someone does not want to continue living. Then, one of the major reasons why it is wrong to kill him disappears. But, remember, even if someone desires to live, the degree to which it is bad to kill him depends very heavily on how many desires he has about his future life. The more goals he has that will remain unfulfilled, the worse it is to take his life. On this approach, the morality of killing is strongly dependent on the individual's desires.

Other Consequences Have To Be Taken into Account.   The wrongness of killing and the rightness of life-saving depends primarily on the good or bad consequences that result from those actions. This means that, in any given case, a killing may be right even if it greatly frustrates the desires of the victim, if there are other good consequences that outweigh this frustration of desire. It also means that it may be wrong to save the life of a person, even if that leads to much desire satisfaction for that person, because saving his life may have bad consequences for other people. None of this should be a surprise, for this is precisely what we mean when we say that utilitarians are consequentialists and believe that nothing is intrinsically right or intrinsically wrong.

Means Don't Count.   We saw in Chapter 9 that some people think it is important to distinguish between actively taking someone's life and passively failing to save a life. Our utilitarian analysis must reject this distinction as having no moral significance. After all, according to it, only the consequences of an act are important, and the consequences of killing are the same as the consequences of letting someone die. In either case the person ends up dead. Thus, the utilitarian must reject the significance of this distinction.

In the remaining sections of this chapter, we will see how this basic utilitarian approach, with its fundamental corollaries, leads to important conclusions about the life and death issues with which we are concerned.

10·2 A UTILITARIAN ANALYSIS OF SUICIDE AND EUTHANASIA

The utilitarian analysis we offer in this section leads to three major conclusions:

1. All the standard arguments concerning suicide and euthanasia which we summarized in section 9.2 are totally irrelevant in determining when, if ever, suicide or euthanasia is morally permissible.
2. There is an objective standard for the rightness or wrongness of any contemplated act of suicide or euthanasia, and it is to some degree independent of the desires of the person who is to die.
3. Such distinctions as causing death vs. letting it occur and voluntary vs. involuntary euthanasia have much less significance than is normally attributed to them.

Let's examine how utilitarianism has arrived at each of these highly controversial conclusions.

The standard argument for the moral permissibility of suicide is that people have the right to do with their lives as they see best. Utilitarians reject this argument, as they reject all arguments which appeal to the rights of individuals. The standard argument against suicide is that the person is failing to fulfill his obligations, either to other people, to society, or to God. Utilitarians also reject this argument, as they reject all arguments which appeal to special obligations that individuals have. The standard argument for voluntary euthanasia is that a person has the right to ask to be killed and that someone else has the right to honor that request. As with suicide, utilitarians reject this argument as they reject all arguments which appeal to individuals' rights. And so on. . . . The point should be obvious: All the standard arguments for or against suicide or euthanasia are based on conceptions of who has what rights and who is under what obligations. Utilitarianism, as a consequentialist mode of thinking, must therefore reject all these standard arguments.

What, then, is the standard by which utilitarians evaluate proposed acts of suicide or euthanasia? It is their usual standard that an action is right if it leads to the best consequences and wrong if it does not. Thus, an act of suicide or euthanasia will be morally right when it leads to the most satisfaction and least frustration of desires. When an act of suicide or euthanasia fails to achieve these results, it will be morally impermissible.

To illustrate, consider the case of someone who is contemplating suicide because he is terminally ill and does not want to endure the pain and indignity of a slow death. Suppose, moreover, it is quite certain that the continued existence of this person will not produce any important benefits for his family or his society. In this case, utilitarians will claim that suicide is the right thing to do. After all, his continued existence will frustrate his important desire to avoid pain and indignity, and there are no counter balancing desires which his continued existence will satisfy. In sum, because his death will lead to better consequences than will his continued existence, causing his death is therefore the right thing to do.

Notice that the conclusion drawn here allows no distinction between suicide and euthanasia. Moreover, it does not distinguish voluntary from involuntary euthanasia. In short, then, under the circumstances we have drawn, the utilitarian point of view says there is little difference between suicide, voluntary euthanasia, and involuntary euthanasia.

Now let us imagine a different set of circumstances. In this case, someone is contemplating suicide because he has suffered a setback which makes him feel that life is no longer worth living. But here, despite what he thinks, his death will not lead to the best consequences. This person's temporary unhappiness is causing him to misjudge the quality of the rest of his life. If he continues to exist, he will be able to restructure his life so that many important desires (while perhaps momentarily forgotten) will be satisfied. Since his death now will lead to frustration of these desires, the utilitarian may conclude that causing his death, whether he does it himself or someone else does it, is morally wrong.

It is important to notice that in one of these cases the utilitarian agrees that what the person wants to do is morally right while, in the other case, he views the person's choice as morally wrong. Recall that from the utilitarian point of view, the desires of the person are important because they help determine whether his continued existence will lead to more satisfaction or more frustration of desires. Nevertheless, the person's desire to continue living does not settle the matter. As our second case shows, the utilitarian analysis may well conclude that in some cases suicide or euthanasia is wrong. In this respect, the utilitarian approach demands an appraisal of each situation that must be to some degree independent of the desires and decisions of the individual in question.

Another important consideration in these cases is what implications the particular death has for the satisfaction or frustration of other people's desires. If, for example, there is some reason to expect that the terminally ill person is going to make an important contribution to the lives of others, then the utilitarian may well conclude that it would be wrong for the person to commit suicide or to request that another person take his life. The frustration of his own desires brought about by his continued existence may be outweighed by the benefits that his life will confer upon others. By the same reasoning, we can conclude that if new evidence on the person in our second example suggests that his continued existence will have an extremely negative impact on the lives of others, then the utilitarian may have to conclude that his suicide or someone else's act of voluntary euthanasia is justified. This is another example of the way in which the utilitarian criterion for judging the rightness or wrongness of suicide or euthanasia is to some degree independent of the desires of the party in question.

These two points help bring out the third major conclusion of the utilitarian analysis of suicide and euthanasia. To illustrate, let's consider once more the case of the person who is terminally ill. Suppose that the utilitarian concludes, as he often will in such cases, that the person is right in choosing to die. This conclusion rests upon the implications of the person's continued existence, both for himself and for others. Therefore, it usually will not make a difference who takes his life — or how it is taken. In other words, in such cases, utilitarians will approve the person's causing his own death (suicide) and someone else's causing his death (euthanasia), either actively by killing him or passively by doing nothing to stop him from dying. In the second case, where the person has suffered a great reverse and wants to die, and where the utilitarian concludes, as he often will in such cases, that the person is wrong in choosing to die, the implications are parallel. Any manner of killing will be considered wrong here, whether it comes about by the person's own hand (suicide) or by way of others (euthanasia), and whether it is done actively or results from passive nonprevention.

In short, then, the utilitarian analysis places at the forefront the question of whether the particular person will be better off alive or dead, and whether others will be better off with him alive or dead. The utilitarian will find all forms of life-taking wrong except where the person's death will produce the best results, taking into account the interests of all concerned. Thus, for the utilitarian, the moral quality of the act of taking a human life depends on the quality of that life for the person who must live it and the implications of his living for others who are affected by him.

10·3 A UTILITARIAN ANALYSIS OF ABORTION

When we examined the issue of abortion in section 9.3, we saw that all the standard discussions of this subject focus on two major questions.

One is whether the fetus is a human being with a right to life as compelling as the right to life that people already born have, and the other is what implications for the moral permissibility of abortion derive from determining the fetus's status — and thereby its right to life.

Based on what we have learned so far about the utilitarian approach to moral problems, it is clear that utilitarian thinkers will not base their analysis of abortion on these sorts of considerations. After all, the presupposition of the standard discussion is that the moral permissibility of abortion is determined by the rights of the woman and the rights, if any, of the fetus. The utilitarian approach, however, does not recognize the legitimacy of this analysis of moral problems. Instead, it demands that abortion be examined solely in terms of its consequences. Thus, a specific act of abortion will be morally permissible if it leads to a maximization of the satisfaction of desires; otherwise, it will not be morally permissible. In general, then, the utilitarian dismisses the standard discussions about the moral permissibility of abortion in much the same way he dismisses most of the standard arguments about the moral permissibility of suicide and euthanasia.

To examine the problem of abortion from the utilitarian perspective, we must first deal with a question that is fundamental to this analysis. Put very simply, it is this: In assessing the consequences of an abortion, should we only take into account the consequences for those already born, or should we also consider the consequences for the fetus? In particular:

1. In assessing the consequences of not having the abortion, should we include the consequences for the fetus of its continuing existence?
2. In assessing the consequences of having the abortion, should we consider any losses and/or gains that may come to the fetus from its ceasing to exist?

It seems likely that the utilitarian would answer these two questions differently. If the woman does not have an abortion, then the fetus will exist, and some of its desires will be met while others will be frustrated. Its existence, with a particular quality of life, is a consequence that should be weighed. If its quality of life would be high — in the sense that its life would contain much more desire satisfaction than desire frustration — then that is a favorable consequence of not having the abortion, and it should be weighed accordingly. If, on the other hand, the fetus's quality of life would be low — that is, if its life would contain much more frustration of desire than satisfaction of desire — then this is an unfavorable consequence of not having the abortion, and it should be weighed on the side which says that it is wrong not to have the abortion. However, in determining the consequences of having an abortion (at least until such time as the fetus may begin to have desires), we should not take into account what the fetus's life would have been like had it continued, because if the fetus is destroyed it will not have had desires, and nothing will have been satisfied or frustrated. From the utilitarian point of view, all that we are concerned with is maximizing the satisfaction of desires and minimizing the frustration of desires.

Note, however, that other utilitarians view this matter differently. Their feeling is that if the fetus's life would have been of high quality, then this should count as an argument against having an abortion. Their reasoning is that in this case an abortion would not serve the goal of maximizing the satisfaction of desires. For, after all, were the fetus to live, a high quality of life would not be lost and there would be more desire satisfaction in the world. Readers will have to decide for themselves which of these two versions of the utilitarian analysis they prefer.

What are the implications of this theoretical approach, on either version, for the question of abortion? Naturally, no firm moral rules are supportable on the basis of this analysis. Whether an abortion is morally permissible in a given case will depend on the assessment of the consequences of that particular case. Let's look at an example of how such an assessment might be made.

Mrs. Jones is in ill health. Her husband has been laid off his job, and they and their two children are living in very strained economic circumstances. Moreover, Mrs. Jones is in a very early stage of pregnancy (in which the fetus has yet to develop the capacity to have desires), and she is contemplating having an abortion. From the utilitarian point of view, in order to decide whether an abortion is morally permissible, she has to examine the consequences of both having and not having the abortion. If she does not have the abortion, then her continued pregnancy and the resulting birth will have unfortunate consequences for her and her family. One such consequence is that it will aggravate her illness; another is that it will increase the family's financial burden. Thus, for everyone but the fetus, the consequences of not having an abortion are quite bad. The consequences for the fetus, which of course also have to be weighed, are harder to predict. In this case, however, there is some reason to suppose that the gain (if any) to the fetus from its continued existence will not be sufficient to outweigh the loss its continued existence will impose on the mother and the rest of the family. If this is so, then not having an abortion will have a net negative result. If Mrs. Jones has the abortion, she will thereby avoid the bad consequences, which would be the net result of her not having the abortion. Therefore, it would appear that she should have an abortion in such a case.

Notice that in assessing the consequences of *having* the abortion, we did not consider the gains or losses to the fetus from taking its life. We calculated the net results for all who exist (including the fetus) if the woman does *not* have the abortion, but we excluded the fetus from our calculations if she *does* have the abortion. This is because we were following the first of the approaches mentioned above.

Of course, most cases are not this clear-cut. And the utilitarian tells us that here, as in all issues of morality, there are no suitable absolute rules, except for the utilitarian principle itself. Therefore, all we can do is assess the consequences of the fetus's continued existence for the woman, for her family and others who are involved, and for the fetus itself. The decision about the moral permissibility of abortion will depend on this case-by-case analysis of the consequences.

10·4 A UTILITARIAN ANALYSIS OF THE ALLOCATION OF SCARCE MEDICAL RESOURCES

When we first posed the problem of the allocation of scarce medical resources in section 9.4, we presupposed that society would clearly spend whatever is required to save the lives of those whom it can save. The big question that we raised in that section was how to decide whom to save and whom to let die when society is unable to save everyone.

Before we examine what utilitarianism has to say about that question, it is worth noting that utilitarian thinkers would first want us to reexamine the presupposition that we should spend the resources required to save as many lives as we can. Many nonutilitarians simply take this presupposition for granted, either because they believe that human life is sacred and that every effort must therefore be made to save it, or because they believe that everyone has a right to be saved and we must therefore spend whatever is required to accommodate that right. Utilitarians, however, because they are consequentialist moral thinkers, hold neither of those views. From their perspective, saving human lives is a good thing only when the consequences of doing so are, on the whole, better than the consequences of letting people die. It is in this sense that utilitarians might want to challenge the presupposition that we should always strive to save as many lives as we can.

Kidney dialysis is a fine example of an expensive life-saving technique. An example of this issue can be drawn from real experience. Some years ago, Congress passed a law which had the federal government assume the cost of kidney dialysis for all patients requiring it. This law passed with little opposition, although it was clear to everyone that over the years this policy would represent a substantial expenditure. Presumably, in this case, Congress was committed to the standard view that we should save as many lives as possible, whatever the cost.

Utilitarians are suspicious of this wisdom: they wonder, for one thing, whether we couldn't find other, more beneficial ways to use the money. Perhaps, for example, it would be better used to provide food programs to those suffering from malnutrition, or physical therapy to those suffering from multiple sclerosis, or any number of other uses. From the utilitarian point of view, then, it is extremely important that we first examine the question of *whether* to spend the money that is required to provide the life-saving therapy before we examine the question of *whom* to save if we cannot save everyone.

Let us now suppose, for the sake of our analysis, that we have agreed in a given case that it is best to spend the necessary resources to provide some life-saving medical treatment. What does the utilitarian have to say about the three alternatives discussed in section 9.4?

The first view that we presented there was that we should operate on a first come, first served basis. The assumption behind this approach is that everyone has a right to the treatment and that we must provide it to all who come until we are no longer able to provide it. Only then may we turn someone away. Now, it is obvious that utilitarians would reject this argument that everyone has a right to the treatment, for, as we have seen many times, utilitarians do not believe in these rights. Moreover, utilitarians would probably reject the whole first come, first served approach, because it does not analyze the consequences of saving each particular life. If, as seems likely, saving some lives will produce more beneficial consequences than will saving others, then the utilitarian will have to advocate saving the former lives even if the people in question are not the first to request treatment.

The second view that we discussed in section 9.4 was the random-choice approach. The basic argument for this policy is that it is the only way to meet the requirement that everyone be given an equal chance to receive the treatment. Naturally, utilitarians would also reject this argument, since, as consequentialists, they have no commitment to the moral ideal of equality. Moreover, utilitarians would probably reject the whole random-choice approach. After all, it, too, fails to take into account the probability that saving some lives produces better consequences than does saving others. If that is indeed the case, then utilitarians will have to propose the saving of some lives and oppose the saving of others, and they cannot, therefore, accept a random-choice method of allocation.

By the process of elimination, it is fairly clear that utilitarians will have to adopt the third of our approaches, that of weighing the lives in question. Here, we decide whom to save by examining and weighing the gains from saving some lives against the gains from saving others.

We save those whose lives afford the greatest gain. This alternative is completely in the spirit of utilitarianism, and it would clearly be the method of allocation of scarce medical resources adopted by utilitarian thinkers.

10·5 CONCLUSION

A common theme has emerged from this chapter's treatment of our moral problems; that is, utilitarians do not treat every human life as being of the same value. Rather, each life has a greater or lesser value relative to the others depending on the consequences resulting from the continuation of that life. This revolutionary point of view is central to the utilitarian way of thinking about such value questions as suicide, euthanasia, abortion, and the allocation of scarce medical resources. In the next chapter, we will see how a different view on the value of human life leads the deontologist to very different approaches to the resolution of our moral problems.

Exercises

Define in your own words the following terms:

1. utilitarian theory of the wrongness of killing
2. quality of life

Review Questions

1. Why do utilitarians reject the view that killing is intrinsically wrong? In what ways do they nevertheless argue that it is usually wrong?
2. How does the utilitarian approach lead to the conclusion that some killings of innocent people are worse than others?
3. What standards do utilitarians use in evaluating proposed acts of suicide and euthanasia?
4. Why do utilitarians find the active/passive distinction morally irrelevant?
5. In evaluating the consequences of a proposed abortion, what factors is the utilitarian most likely to take into account?

6. Why does utilitarianism reject all the standard approaches to the question of how to allocate scarce medical resources?

7. By what criteria do utilitarians weigh the value of human lives in allocating scarce medical resources?

Questions for Further Thought

1. Is there any way for a hedonistic utilitarian to develop a proper theory of the morality of killing?

2. How would a utilitarian respond to the following objection: "Since you can never be sure about the consequences of your actions, you should never gamble on irrevocable acts. Suicide is the most irrevocable act. Therefore, it is always wrong to commit suicide."

3. At what point (if any) in fetal development does a person start to exist whose desires must be counted in weighing the consequences of having an abortion? What implications does your answer have for the morality of abortions for any reason?

4. Many people have suggested that pregnancies which result from rape are clear-cut cases in which abortion is morally permissible. Evaluate this view from the utilitarian perspective.

5. Many people have suggested that pregnancies in which the fetus is known to be defective are clear-cut cases in which abortion is morally permissible. Evaluate this view from the utilitarian perspective.

6. Evaluate the following utilitarian argument for the random-choice approach: "If we don't adopt the random-choice approach, there will be a great deal of unhappiness because many people will perceive society as acting unfairly. Therefore, the best consequences are really those that result from the random-choice method of scarce resource allocation."

Chapter Eleven

Questions of Life and Death: A Deontological Approach

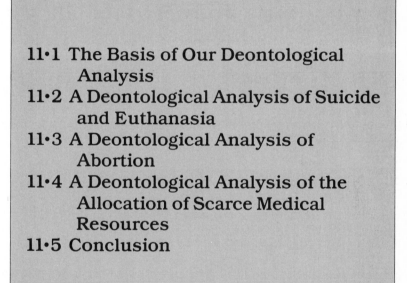

Deontological thinking about questions of life and death centers around the rights of the party whose life is threatened. As we shall see in this chapter, the crucial question from the deontological point of view is, When are the rights of the threatened party to be respected and when may those rights be overridden? Although deontologists agree on this common approach to problems of life and death, they differ on their precise views concerning the rights of the party in question. Therefore, once more it is necessary to caution you to keep in mind that the analysis of this chapter is *a* deontological approach to our moral problems concerning life and death, it is not *the only* deontological approach.

11·1 THE BASIS OF OUR DEONTOLOGICAL ANALYSIS

A phrase that has gained much currency in the last few years is *right to life.* These words have come to imply different things to different people, and because they have fundamental implications for the deontological analysis, let's understand right away what they mean. First, it is extremely important to distinguish two aspects of this right to life. These are:

1. The right not to be killed. This right, which we hold against all other people, is the right that no one may cause our death.
2. The right to receive life-saving aid. This right, which we hold against different people in differing degrees, is the right that others must come to our aid to help save our life.

Second, we must understand precisely what we mean when we say that one person (A) has killed another person (B). In the broadest sense, it means that A has caused the death of B. But there are, of course, many ways in which one can cause the death of someone else. Sometimes it is done by performing certain specific actions, such as poisoning, shooting, or stabbing. Other times it is done by *not* acting, such as neglecting an infant. A parent who fails to feed a child who cannot feed itself, can, simply by continuing to do this, cause the child to die. In other words, when we define killing as causing someone's death, we mean both through action and inaction. The crucial element in killing is causation, not action.

On this analysis of killing, we can see that the right to life consists in part of the right we hold against all other people that they not cause our death. It is important to keep in mind that this right is independent of the specific relationship that holds between us and those other people. We have this right to life against them not because of a special relationship that holds between us and them, but simply because we and they are persons. It is also important to understand that this is an extremely grave right. One way to see this is to keep in mind how few justifications there are available to those who violate this right. Even then, such as in the justification of self-defense, the person must show that no other, less grave option was available. Very few other justifications are available to the person who causes someone's death. The obligation not to cause someone's death takes precedence over almost everything else.

Now, in contrast to this aspect of the right to life is the second aspect, which says that we hold the right against all other people that they come to our aid when it is necessary to save our life. Despite this right, in most cases where it has been ignored and the person has died, it is not being suggested that those who failed to act are killers. For example, if I pass someone who is drowning in the river and I could save his life, then my failing to do so certainly means that I have not fulfilled the right he holds against me to come to his aid. Yet the cause of his death is drowning, not my inaction.

There are, however, other cases of inaction where the distinction between action and causation is very subtle. A good example is death which results from child neglect. Our analysis admits that in neither case do we have the person acting purposely to cause the death of the other party. It also admits that in both cases the life would have been saved had the person acted in the appropriate manner. Nevertheless, we distinguish the two cases by claiming that the mother's inaction is the cause of the child's death, whereas drowning is the cause of death of the man in the river, not any failure to help him. So, again, we come back to the notion of causality as the determining factor in the definition of killing. Causality is a notoriously difficult concept. Moreover, while deontologists have no neat theory of causality to offer, they nevertheless rest their analysis upon their abilities to distinguish these cases.

Some deontologists claim that we hold no such right against strangers that they come to our aid to save our life. According to these people, it is very nice if, in times of need, strangers do come to our aid, and it is very insensitive of them to disregard our need; nevertheless, we do not hold a right to this aid and they do not have an obligation to provide it. The case is different, though, when we have special relationships to people. For example, we do hold such a right against the members of our family, against our friends, and against certain others. And they, in turn, have an obligation to provide us life-saving aid. Strangers, however, have no such obligations.

This is not the view that we adopt for our deontological analysis. We shall suppose that people do hold this right to be saved against all others, and that all people have an obligation to come to our aid to save our life. We will, however, adopt the view that special relationships carry special obligations. Moreover, our right to this aid increases proportionally with the closeness of the relationship. But in all cases, this right is weaker than our right not to be killed. Let's look at each of these points more closely.

What sort of justifications can we give for failing to save someone's life? Suppose that we could only do so at enormous expense, so that all our savings would be wiped out. Would this justify our killing someone? Can we kill an innocent party to save our life savings? Presumably not. However, it also seems clear that we have no obligation to an absolute stranger to give up our life savings in order to save his life, even if it might be a nice thing for us to do. He holds no right against us to such extreme aid. It is very different, of course, with members of our immediate family. Here, they do have a right to that aid and we have an obligation to provide it.

It is contrasts of this sort which suggest (1) that the right not to be killed is more fundamental that the right to be saved; and (2) that we hold a more substantial right to be saved against those with whom we have special relations than against those who are total strangers.

In approaching the moral questions in this chapter, our deontological analysis will employ these fundamental conceptual distinctions. We will have to see which aspect of the right to life is involved: is it the right not to be killed, or the right to be saved? Having answered that question, we will then have to see whether there is any justification for violating the right in question.

11·2 A DEONTOLOGICAL ANALYSIS OF SUICIDE AND EUTHANASIA

The deontologist approaches the problems of suicide and euthanasia with the assumption that the moral question involved is whether these actions violate someone's right not to be killed. From the deontological point of view, cases of suicide and euthanasia are instances in which someone is killed. So the moral question is whether that killing is wrong on the basis that it violates the rights of the party who is killed.

On this analysis, the deontologist has little trouble justifying the moral permissibility of suicide. In every case of suicide, the person whose right to life is being violated is himself the violator. Certainly the person who commits suicide holds a right against everyone that they not take his life, for this is part of what we mean when we talk about that person's right to life. However, in the act of committing suicide, the victim waives this aspect of his right to life. Therefore, his act of suicide is not morally impermissible.

It is important to note several crucial points about this deontological argument:

1. It presupposes that if there is anything intrinsically morally objectionable about committing suicide it is that it violates the victim's right to life. Note that in saying this, the deontologist is
   rejecting the view that suicide is wrong because the person is
   violating the rights of the state (to the contributions he can make)
   or the rights of God (to determine the time and manner of his
   death).

2. In saying that there is nothing intrinsically morally impermissible
   with committing suicide, the deontologist is not suggesting that
   there can be no cases in which committing suicide is wrong. The
   victim may hurt many of the people he leaves behind who depend
   on him, he may leave various obligations unfulfilled, and so forth.
   In these sorts of cases, his action may be morally impermissible
   because, in addition to being an act of self-destruction, it is also an
   act of harming others or of cheating others out of what is due to
   them, or. . . .

3. The crucial final assumption of this argument is that we can waive
   any of our rights, and once we have done so, nobody acts wrongly
   on the grounds that they have violated the waived right.

4. In arguing that acts of suicide are morally permissible, the deontologist is not claiming that such acts are reasonable or wise. People
   often kill themselves for foolish reasons, or impulsively in times of
   stress, despair, or weakness. There are many things which are
   morally permissible to do but which we would be foolish to do. The
   deontologist is merely saying that whatever the wisdom of the
   particular act of suicide, it is nonetheless morally permissible except in those cases in which the person committing suicide thereby
   harms others or fails to fulfill his obligations to others.

There are two ways in which this deontological argument can easily
be extended to justify acts of voluntary euthanasia. First, we can
simply apply the same principles which justify suicide to acts of voluntary euthanasia; second, we can apply principles of agency.

The crux of the deontological argument for the moral permissibility
of suicide is that by consenting to his life being taken, which is implicit
in the act of suicide, the victim thereby waives his right to life. If this is
a valid justification, then it would seem to make no difference who acts
upon that consent—he, or someone else. In either case his consent
legitimizes the act of killing by waiving his right to life. This also brings
out the principle of agency. For example, if, on these grounds, it is
morally permissible for me to take my own life, then it should be
morally permissible for someone else to take my life at my request (to
act as my agent). After all, if I may do something, why can't I appoint
someone else (my agent) to do that thing for me?

In sum, either application of this argument suggests that voluntary euthanasia should be viewed as an extension of suicide; thus, justifications for the moral permissibility of one act are applicable to the other.

Some people claim that the state should not legalize acts of voluntary euthanasia even if it legalizes acts of suicide. Their reasoning is that it is too hard to tell when an act of euthanasia is truly voluntary, because in some cases it is difficult to detect fraud. This is an important consideration, and one which must be weighed carefully in considering whether the state should legalize voluntary euthanasia by making the consent of the victim a defense against charges of homicide. That important legal question is not, however, relevant to our present discussion. Our concern here is with the moral permissibility of individual acts of voluntary euthanasia.

What about involuntary euthanasia? From the deontological point of view, this is an entirely different matter. Any act of involuntary euthanasia seems to violate the person's right not to be killed, since, by virtue of its being involuntary, the person has not waived his right. It would seem, therefore, that the deontologist would always be opposed to involuntary euthanasia. But there is another factor which needs to be taken into account. Sometimes we feel very confident that the person in question would waive his right to life by requesting that he be killed if he were able to do so. In the case of Karen Quinlan, for example, her family and friends were quite certain that she would have requested euthanasia if she could have. In such cases, the deontologist might well be willing to argue that the hypothetical consent of the person, the consent he would give if he could, is sufficient to nullify his right to life. Thus, for this limited class of acts, the deontologist would consider involuntary euthanasia morally permissible.

Notice that we have said nothing about the distinction between active and passive suicide or between active and passive euthanasia. The moral permissibility of suicide and voluntary euthanasia (and of certain cases of involuntary euthanasia) derives from the consent (occasionally hypothetical) of the victim and extends, as long as the victim has consented, to the active taking of his life and to the passive failure to save his life. If this distinction is to have any significance at all, it will have to be in those cases of involuntary euthanasia in which the deontologist concludes that the active euthanasia is morally impermissible.

In comparing the intuitionist analysis of our moral problems with the utilitarian analysis, which was presented in section 10.2, we see that these approaches are diametrically opposite. Unlike the utilitarian, the deontologist agrees with many of the standard arguments about suicide and euthanasia (refer back to section 9.2). Deontology, moreover, says that the standard for judging the rightness or wrongness of any contemplated act of suicide or euthanasia depends heavily on the victim's desires; it is totally independent of *our* judgment of the value of that person's life. Another difference is that the deontologist, unlike the utilitarian, places great significance on such distinctions as that between voluntary and involuntary euthanasia and that between active and passive killing.

11·3 A DEONTOLOGICAL ANALYSIS OF ABORTION

When we examined the question of abortion in section 9.3, we saw that all the standard discussions focus on two major issues. One is whether the fetus is a human being with a right to life as strong as that of people already born. The other is what implications there are for the moral permissibility of abortion of whatever right to life the fetus has. Utilitarianism, as we saw in section 10.3, rejects this whole standard approach. Deontology, however, accepts it and bases its argument within that standard framework.

The question which deontology must consider first is that of fetal humanity. Some argue that the fetus is a human being with a right to life (or, for convenience, just a human being) from the moment of conception. Others argue that the fetus only becomes a human being at the moment of birth. Many positions in between these two extremes have also been suggested. How are we to decide which is correct?

The analysis which we will propose here rests upon certain metaphysical assumptions, which are summarized by the following argument: (a) The question is, When does the fetus acquire all the properties essential (necessary) for being a human being? For when it has, it is a human being; (b) Essential properties are defined as those without which the human being goes out of existence; (c) Human beings go out of existence when they die. Thus, the fetus becomes a human being when it acquires all the characteristics that are essential to life; the loss of any one of these characteristics results in death.

Traditionally, death has been defined in terms of a cessation of cardiac and respiratory activity. Doctors would test for such cessation by using mirrors to detect emission of breath and by seeking the pulse to detect continued circulation. It was recognized that death could also be brought about by the destruction of other systems and organs (the liver, the kidneys, the brain), but it was generally thought that their destruction caused death indirectly by affecting the functioning of the heart and lung. In recent years, there has been a growing tendency to replace this traditional view with the definition of death as an irreparable cessation of brain function rather than a cessation of cardiac and respiratory activity.

As we define the concept of death to help determine what is essential for being human, we must remember that there remain some fundamental questions to which deontologists are unable to give precise answers. This is not surprising in light of the complexity of human life. We will first consider the question of what properties are essential to being human from the view that death and the passing out of existence occur only when there has been an irreparable cessation of brain function (the brain-death theory). We shall then consider the same question from the view that death occurs only when the brain, heart, and lung all have irreparably ceased to function (the modified traditional theory).

According to what is called the *brain-death theory,* as long as there has not been an irreparable cessation of brain function the person in question continues to exist, no matter what else has happened to him. On this view, it seems to follow that there is only one property — leaving aside those entailed by this property — that is essential to humanity, namely, the possession of a brain that has not suffered an irreparable cessation of function.

Let us now look at the following argument: (1) A functioning brain (or at least a brain that, if not functioning, is susceptible of function) is a property that every human being must have because it is essential for being human. (2) By the time a fetus acquires that property, it has all the other properties that are essential for being human. (3) Therefore, when the fetus acquires a functioning brain (by about six weeks after conception), it becomes a human being.

But what if we reject the brain-death theory and replace it with its equally plausible contender, the *modified traditional theory*? On this view, the human being does not die — does not go out of existence — until such time as the brain, heart, and lungs have irreparably ceased functioning naturally. What are the essential features of being human according to this theory?

Actually, the adoption of this theory requires no major modifications. What is essential to being human — that is, what each human being must retain if he is to continue to exist — is the possession of a functioning (actually or potentially) heart, lung, or brain. Thus, the fetus comes into humanity, so to speak, when it acquires any one of these organs.

On the modified traditional theory, the argument would now run as follows: (1) A functioning brain, heart, or lung (or at least those that, if not functioning, are susceptible of function) is a property that every human being must have because it is essential for being human. (2) By the time a fetus acquires that property, it has all the other properties that are essential for being human. (3) Therefore, when the fetus acquires a functioning heart (the first of these organs to function, by about three to six weeks after conception), it becomes a human being.

While we have not reached a precise answer to the question of when the fetus becomes a human being, we do know that it happens some-time between the middle of the third week (when the heart first begins to flutter) and the end of the second month (when brain activity can first be detected). Thus, we have narrowed considerably the range of acceptable answers.

Now that we know approximately when the fetus becomes a human being — and thereby acquires the same right to life as people already born — we must look at the implications this holds for the moral permissibility of abortion.

Let's begin the deontological analysis of this question by considering a case in which the continued existence of the fetus threatens the life of the mother. It would seem that the mother then has the strongest claim for the right to abort the fetus, even if it is a human being with a right to life. Since the fetus's continued existence poses a threat to her life, killing the fetus by having an abortion may be considered an ultimate act of self-defense.

To be sure, it may be a physician or other agent who causes the fetus's death, and not the mother herself, but to the deontologist, that difference is irrelevant. After all, the person whose life is threatened (person A) may either kill the person who threatens her life (person B), or she may call upon someone else (person C) to do it for her. And it seems permissible for C to take B's life in order to save A's life. Put in traditional terms, we are really speaking of the mother's right as the pursued, or anyone else's right as an onlooker, to take the life of the fetus who is the pursuer.

This whole matter of pursuit requires, however, a more careful examination. Let us imagine that there is a medicine that A needs to stay alive. D owns some, and D will give it to A only if A kills B. Moreover, A has no other way of getting the medicine. In this case, the continued existence of B certainly poses a threat to the life of A. A can survive only if B does not survive. Still, it is not permissible for A to kill B in order to save A's life. Why not? How does this case differ from a normal case of killing the pursuer? The simplest answer is that in this case, while B's continued existence poses a threat to the life of A, B is not guilty of attempting to take A's life because there is no attempt to be guilty about it in the first place. Now if we consider the case of a fetus whose continued existence poses a threat to the life of the mother, we see that it is like the medicine case and not like the normal case of killing the pursuer. The fetus does pose (in our imagined situation) a threat to the life of its mother, but it is not guilty of attempting to take its mother's life. Consequently, in an analogue to the medicine case, the mother (or her agent) could not justify destroying the fetus on the ground that it would be a permissible act of killing the pursuer.

The persuasiveness of both the preceding arguments indicates that we have to analyze the whole issue of pursuit far more carefully before we can definitely decide whether an abortion to save the life of the mother could be viewed as a permissible act of killing the pursuer. If we look again at a normal case of pursuit, we see that there are three factors involved:

1. The continued existence of B poses a threat to the life of A, a threat that can be met only by the taking of B's life (we shall refer to this as the *condition of danger*).
2. B is unjustly attempting to take A's life (we shall refer to this as the *condition of attempt*).
3. B is responsible for his attempt to take A's life (we shall refer to this as the *condition of guilt*).

In the medicine case, only the danger condition was satisfied. Our intuitions that it would be wrong for A to take B's life in that case reflect our belief that the mere fact that B is a danger to A is not sufficient to establish that killing B will be a justifiable act of killing a pursuer. But it would be rash to conclude that all three conditions must be satisfied before the killing of B will be a justifiable act of killing a pursuer. What would happen, for example, if the first two conditions, but not the guilt condition, were satisfied?

There are good reasons for supposing that the satisfaction of the first two conditions is sufficient justification for taking B's life as an act of killing the pursuer. Consider, for example, a variation of a pursuit paradigm — one in which B is about to shoot A, and the only way A can stop him is by killing him first — but one in which B is a minor who is not responsible for his attempt to take A's life. In this case, the only condition not satisfied is the condition of guilt. Still, despite that fact, it seems that A may justifiably take B's life as a permissible act of killing a pursuer. The guilt of the pursuer, then, is not a requirement for legitimacy in killing the pursuer.

Are there any cases in which the satisfaction of the danger condition and something weaker than the attempt condition is sufficient to justify A's killing B as an act of killing a pursuer? It seems that there may be. Consider, for example, the following case: B is about to press a button that turns on a light, and there is no reason for him to suspect that his doing so will also explode a bomb that will destroy A. Moreover, the only way in which we can stop B and save A's life is by taking B's life, for there is no opportunity to warn B of the actual consequences of his act. In such a case, B is not attempting to take A's life and, thus, he is neither responsible for nor guilty of any such attempt. Nevertheless, this may still be a case in which there is justification for taking B's life in order to save A's life; that is, this may still be a legitimate case of killing a pursuer.

How does this case differ from the medicine case? Or, to put our question another way, What condition, in addition to the danger condition, is satisfied in this case but not in the medicine case, so that its satisfaction (together with the satisfaction of the danger condition) is sufficient to justify our killing B as an act of killing a pursuer? As we think about the two cases, the following idea suggests itself: There is, in this most recent example, some action that B is doing (pressing the button) that will result in A's death, an action that if taken in full knowledge and voluntarily would result in B's being responsible for the loss of A's life. Even if performed without full knowledge and intent, this action itself justifies the taking of B's life. In the medicine case, on the other hand, no such action is performed. D may well be to blame for the loss of A's life if he does not give A the medicine when A refuses to kill B. But this has nothing to do with B. It would seem, then, that A is justified in taking B's life as an act of killing a pursuer if, in addition to B's being a danger to A, the following condition is satisfied:

2′. B is doing some action that will lead to A's death, and that action is such that if B were a responsible person who did it voluntarily, knowing that this result would come about, B would be responsible for the loss of A's life (we shall refer to this as the *condition of action*).

To summarize our general discussion of killing the pursuer, we can say the following: The mere satisfaction of the danger condition is not sufficient to justify the killing of the pursuer. If, in addition, either the attempt condition or the condition of action is satisfied, then one would be justified in killing the pursuer to save the life of the pursued. In any case, the condition of guilt, arising from full knowledge and intent, need not be satisfied.

Let us return now to the problem of abortion and apply these results to the case of the fetus whose continued existence poses a threat to the life of its mother. Is it permissible, as an act of killing a pursuer, to abort the fetus in order to save the mother? It is true that in such cases the fetus is a danger to its mother. But it is also clear that the condition of attempt is not satisfied. The fetus has neither the beliefs nor the intentions to which we have referred. Furthermore, there is on the part of the fetus no action that threatens the life of the mother. So not even the condition of action is satisfied. It seems to follow, therefore, that aborting the fetus could not be a permissible act of killing a pursuer; and that if the fetus is a human being with the same right to life as all other human beings, the abortion would not be morally permissible even to save the life of the mother.

Our deontological analysis concludes, then, that from a relatively early stage in fetal development, abortions are almost never morally permissible.

11·4 A DEONTOLOGICAL ANALYSIS OF THE ALLOCATION OF SCARCE MEDICAL RESOURCES

The question of the allocation of scarce medical resources is one of deciding whom to save when we cannot save everyone. As such, what is at stake is the right to be saved rather than the right not to be killed. In this respect, this last question is fundamentally different from the problems of suicide, euthanasia, and abortion.

As we pointed out in section 11.1, some deontological thinkers do not concur with the belief that we have the right to receive life-saving aid and that others have a corresponding obligation to provide that aid. But the analysis in this chapter presupposes both these beliefs. We will, therefore, try to resolve the moral question of the allocation of scarce medical resources in terms of this right to receive aid.

We saw in section 11.1 that the right to receive aid required to save our life is very different from the right not to be killed. The most crucial difference, for our present purpose, is that we hold a more substantial right to be saved against those to whom we stand in special relations than we do against those who are total strangers to us. Similarly, those to whom we stand in special relations have a correspondingly greater obligation to aid us than do those to whom we are total strangers.

Imagine, then, that you are the director of a hospital at which a new life-saving technique has been developed. There are many more applicants in need of the technique and who can be aided by it than the technique can serve. Each applicant comes claiming a right to receive aid and an obligation on your part to save him. How shall you determine which applicants to admit and which to turn away?

If all the claimants are strangers, then you, your hospital, and the society which has provided the resources to build the hospital and to develop the new technique have no special obligations to any of the people. In such a case, they all hold an equal right against you to be saved, and you have an equal obligation to each of them to render aid. It would seem that you must choose either on a first come, first served basis or by a method of random choice.

If, however, not all the claimants are total strangers, then you, or the hospital, or the society may have certain obligations to various parties. For example, you may have an obligation of gratitude for the contributions that some of them have made to society; or an obligation to take care of the children who would be left orphaned if you did not save their parents; and so on. It is unlikely that, in the real world, you would have an equal obligation to all the claimants; and it is equally unlikely that each would have an equal right to the aid. That being the case, neither the first come, first served method nor the method of random choice seems appropriate.

At this point, there is little more that the deontologist can offer by way of providing a general formula for dealing with such cases. The various individual and social obligations to the claimants have to be weighed in each case, and then you must save those to whom you have the greatest obligations and who hold the greatest right against you.

It is interesting to note that both the utilitarians and the deontologists reject the random choice and the first come, first served approaches. However, this does not mean that they agree on how to resolve the problem of the allocation of scarce medical resources. The utilitarian will weigh the lives in question and then save those lives whose continued existence represents the greatest social gain. The deontologist will examine the obligations he has to each of the claimants and then aid those who hold against him the greatest right to be saved. These are clearly very different approaches to the problem.

11·5 CONCLUSION

A common theme has emerged from this chapter's treatment of our moral problems; that is, deontologists are concerned with people's rights to life, not with weighing the value of a human life. They view all people as having an equal right not to be killed, but they recognize differences in people's rights to receive aid. These differences, however, are never based on judgments about the value of a human life, only on the relationships that prescribe the degree to which one holds that right.

Exercises

Define in your own words the following terms:

1. right to life
2. right not to be killed
3. right to aid
4. definition of killing
5. principle of agency in voluntary euthanasia
6. hypothetical consent
7. traditional definition of death
8. brain-death definition of death

9. modified traditional theory of death
10. condition of danger
11. condition of attempt
12. condition of guilt
13. condition of action

Review Questions

1. What are the major components of the right to life? Are there important respects in which they differ in significance?
2. How do deontologists argue for the right to suicide? What are the major presuppositions of that argument?
3. Why do deontologists support voluntary euthanasia? Are there any conditions in which they support involuntary euthanasia?
4. What is the main argument for fetal humanity shortly after conception?
5. Can abortion ever be justified as an act of self-defense?
6. Which component of the right to life is involved in questions of allocating scarce medical resources? What implications does the deontologist draw from that answer?
7. In what ways does the deontologist avoid the weighing of human lives done by the utilitarian?

Questions for Further Thought

1. What sort of arguments would you offer for and against the view that we hold a right against strangers that they come to our aid to save our life?
2. Neither the utilitarian nor the deontological approach seems to find any moral difference between suicide and voluntary euthanasia. Are there any reasons why the law might nevertheless treat them differently?
3. A very popular alternative to the approach adopted in section 11.3 is the view that a fetus has a right to life only at that time (usually after birth) at which it has a definite conception of itself as a continuing entity with a desire to continue to exist. How would this view lead to different conclusions than the conclusions arrived at in this chapter? What are the strengths and weaknesses of this alternative view?
4. Some have argued that even if the fetus has a right to life, abortions are permissible because the fetus is occupying the body of the woman against her desire. Is this an effective argument in all cases? What about in the case of a fetus conceived through rape?

5. How would you analyze those rare cases in which both fetus and woman will die if there is no abortion but in which at least one can be saved if there is an abortion?

6. What is wrong with the following objection: "We all have an equal right to life, so there can be no moral justification for saving some lives and neglecting others."

Chapter Twelve

Autonomy and Paternalism: Some Value Problems

Our final set of value problems centers around questions of decision making, particularly, questions of who should make decisions for whom. We will examine a variety of these questions as they arise in the relationship between a physician, a patient, and society. However, the fundamental issues at hand also arise in many other areas, and it should not be hard for the reader to generalize from this medical context to other contexts.

12·1 THE BASIC CONCEPTS

There are many ways in which we treat children differently from adults. Adults have certain privileges (for example, to vote, to marry, to spend their money as they please) which children do not. Similarly, adults have many responsibilities (for example, to support themselves, to fulfill their contractual obligations) which children do not.

One of the crucial ways in which we treat children differently from adults is in the area of decision making. Adults, usually parents, are expected to make many important decisions for children. They decide how their children will be brought up, how they shall be educated, where they shall live, and so on. The adult is called upon to make these and other important decisions for the child, even though such decisions have profound implications for the child's whole life. Furthermore, especially if the child is quite young, the adult may not even consult with the child first. Such practice is commonplace. We expect it. But we do not normally expect this sort of behavior to take place between adults. We expect adults to make their own decisions, especially the important ones.

This thesis sounds rather straightforward, but it raises some important questions. For example, at what age does the parental privilege end? That is, at what age should children be treated as adults and expected to make their own decisions and assume their own responsibilities? Are some adults so incompetent that they need to be treated as children? By what standards are we to judge them? While these questions hold important implications, they are irrelevant to this discussion. For our present purposes, we need only recognize the broad distinction between adults who are expected to make their own decisions and children for whom we expect others to make decisions.

Along with the privilege of making decisions for one's children goes the responsibility of making them in a way that will benefit those for whom the decisions are made. Thus, parents who consistently make decisions that have harmful consequences for their children risk losing their decision-making privilege by having society revoke it. Children are not property, and they may not be exploited. Decision making on their behalf is not an unconditional or inalienable right: it may be taken away if parents do not fulfill their responsibility to make decisions which will be beneficial for their children.

We call the pattern by which parents and/or other adults make decisions for the benefit of children *paternalistic decision making*. In contrast, the pattern of decision making in which adults make decisions for themselves is called *autonomous decision making*. By these terms we can now speak of the problems which shall concern us in this and the next two chapters as those which center around paternalistic vs. autonomous decision making. Specifically, When are we justified in applying the pattern of paternalistic decision making to another adult, so that one adult (A) is making decisions for another adult (B) in light of A's conception of what is best for B?

Under what circumstances is it legitimate to extend a pattern of decision making developed for handling children to the handling of adults? Most people would suggest that it is legitimate in those situations where one person is clearly competent to make a particular decision and the other is clearly incompetent to make that decision. One possible example is the medical context. Since intelligent decision making in this area often calls for information and abilities that most adults do not possess, we are tempted to allow adults who are expert in the field to make decisions for the benefit of adults who are not.

Throughout this chapter we will describe four areas of medicine in which society is tempted to allow paternalistic rather than autonomous decision making. We will provide some background information that will enable us to examine the relevant issues. Then, following our usual format, the next two chapters will look at these issues from both the utilitarian and deontological perspectives.

12·2 REQUIRING MEDICAL TREATMENT

The first area we shall consider pertains to cases in which an adult clearly requires medical treatment to live but either refuses that treatment or places conditions on the treatment such that the physician is unable to provide it. Our value problem is to decide whether the physician and society in general should allow the adult patient to refuse the treatment (make an autonomous decision) or revoke the patient's privilege to make an autonomous decision in this case and provide the treatment against his will (a paternalistic decision).

This situation frequently arises in the case of Jehovah's Witnesses. A tenet of their faith forbids blood transfusions, no matter what the emergency. Therefore, the question arises as to whether a Jehovah's Witness should be allowed to decide for himself to refuse a transfusion, even though such a decision means that he will die, or whether society should decide, on the basis of its own values, that it is best for the person to receive the life-saving transfusion and authorize a physician to treat the patient without his consent.

Cases of this sort have come before the courts many times. In general, when the patient is a minor and it is the parents who are refusing to allow a blood transfusion, the courts have authorized the physician to do what he thinks best for the child. Thus, in effect, the courts have substituted the physician's paternalistic judgment for the parents' paternalistic judgment. These cases raise many interesting questions, such as, Whose paternalistic decisions should take precedence, those of the parents, in whose judgment the child's interests are best served by refusing a blood transfusion on religious grounds, or those of society, in whose judgment the child's interests are best served by requiring a blood transfusion on the basis of medical opinion that it is necessary in order to save his life? Our concern here, however, is with a different question; namely, Should an adult be allowed to make his own autonomous decisions or should society be allowed to make a paternalistic judgment? In cases where an adult Jehovah's Witness has refused medical treatment on religious grounds, there has been much less unanimity in the courts. Some judges, stressing the right of an adult of sound mind to make his own choices based on his own beliefs, have allowed patients to refuse medical treatment on religious grounds, even though, in many cases, the patient subsequently dies. Other judges, stressing the obligation of physicians and society to preserve human life whenever possible, have revoked the right to autonomous decisions in these cases.

To Jehovah's Witnesses, having a blood transfusion is a sin. Some judges who have decided to respect the patient's wishes, have treated these cases in terms of the issue of religious freedom, not in terms of the issue of an adult's right to be autonomous. Other judges who have reached the same conclusion have treated autonomy as the crucial issue. They have no doubt that the reason why the patient refuses treatment is because of his religious beliefs. However, they see that behind this decision lies the real issue of whether an adult has the right to make his own, autonomous decisions on the basis of whatever beliefs and values he holds.

Of course there are other cases which are not based on religious beliefs that involve the same issue. These cases, which are of increasing public interest, concern the right to refuse medical treatment and the right to "die a dignified death."

Among the tremedous advances in medical technology is the capability of prolonging life through artificial means. But heroic life-saving techniques are not always desired by those to whom they are administered. In these cases, the patient is well aware that he will not be able to live much longer and that the technique simply offers him a somewhat extended span of life in the hospital. To many, this modest and limited extension of life is not worth the loss of dignity they experience by being totally dependent on machinery and by requiring constant care. Moreover, this heroic medical effort is accompanied by a substantial bill, which often places a tremendous financial strain on the patient's family for years to come. For these reasons, many people who find themselves in this type of situation prefer not to be kept alive. Yet physicians and others involved often insist on the continuation of these life-saving measures despite the patients' wishes.

So here we have the same issue but without the religious under-pinnings: Who shall make the decision for whom? Shall the patient be allowed to decide for himself whether or not to prolong his life artifi-cially? Or shall his family or physician be allowed to decide this ques-tion for him? These and similar questions pose difficult legal and moral problems for society as well as for private, individual decision makers.

12·3 PROHIBITING THE USE OF LAETRILE

No one is free of the fear of cancer. Despite the best efforts of modern research, there is still so little that can be done for so many of its victims. Partly for this reason, and partly because dying from cancer can be a long and painful process, it is not surprising that cancer patients often turn to unorthodox therapies when traditional methods seem to offer little help. One of the most publicized of these unorthodox therapies is treatment with Laetrile, a drug extracted from apricot pits. Because test after test has failed to indicate any therapeutic benefit from taking Laetrile, its production and distribution is prohibited in U.S. interstate commerce under the Pure Food and Drug Act. Con-sequently, those who wish to take Laetrile must either obtain a supply illegally or go to some country (most commonly, Mexico) where they can obtain it legally.

It is interesting and important to note the provisions of the Pure Food and Drug Act. The initial Act of 1906 served only to protect consumers against fraudulent, misrepresentative labeling. The Sher-ley Amendment of 1912 increased consumer protection by prohibiting false claims about a drug's therapeutic effects. The more recent amendments of 1962 went still further by requiring that producers and distributors be able to demonstrate both the safety and effective-ness of a drug before it is marketed. It is this very strong statute and its application to the production and distribution of Laetrile which raises, in an extremely direct fashion, our current value questions of au-tonomy and paternalism. Let's look at this more closely.

In some states, statutes have been enacted which legalize the use of Laetrile within that individual state providing that the drug is produced and marketed there. (Note, parenthetically, that it cannot be. The purpose of these statutes is simply an expression of opposition to the federal statute on the part of those who wish to use Laetrile.) In the state of Indiana, for example, a person requesting Laetrile for therapy must sign a form saying (1) that he knows the Food and Drug Administration (FDA) has banned the manufacture and distribution of Laetrile, (2) that he understands that Laetrile is not recommended for use by the generally recognized medical societies, and (3) that he is aware of the alternative forms of treatment that his physician has available. In this way, the Indiana statute ensures that the person requesting Laetrile is not a victim of fraud: He knows what the orthodox medical opinion is but wishes to be treated with Laetrile anyway. The current Pure Food and Drug Act, however, says that he cannot be treated with Laetrile, for it specifies that no one can be treated with a drug until it has been proven safe and effective. Embodied in this Act, then, is society's judgment that an individual ought not to be allowed to make his own autonomous judgment about the advisability of the use of Laetrile and other drugs. This is an obvious example of society applying paternalistic decision making to adults, and it clearly raises the question of paternalism vs. autonomy.

Those who defend the Pure Food and Drug Act and its ban on the use of Laetrile might well argue as follows. Normally, when an adult wants to act in some way that he judges to be in his own interest, then, if no one else will be harmed, society should allow that action, even if most people believe that he will be hurt rather than benefited. We defer to the person's autonomous decision because we assume that adults are the best judges of what is best for them. However, there are certain instances in which this assumption is unlikely to be true—cases in which the individual is operating under conditions of stress, fear, and anxiety which inhibit his normal capacity to make rational judgments. In these situations, society has an obligation to step in and act in a paternalistic fashion to protect the individual from himself. People diagnosed as having cancer are likely to require this sort of protection. After all, a diagnosis of cancer is still widely perceived as equivalent to being sentenced to a slow and painful death. Thus, cancer victims are especially prone to misguided decision making and in need of protection. Among other things, they need to be protected against their own free decision to use Laetrile.

Those who oppose the ban on Laetrile see things differently. They believe that it is enough to have a statute, like the Indiana statute, which simply ensures that anyone requesting Laetrile is not a victim of fraudulent advertising. They object to the federal ban on the use of Laetrile, even when all conditions of the Indiana statute are fulfilled, on the grounds that if, in light of all this information, an adult still chooses to gamble on Laetrile rather than follow the orthodox medical opinion, then we should respect his choice. These opponents of the ban on Laetrile argue that once we start making choices for adults in some situations—because of the stress under which they are operating, for example—there is no stopping the inevitable march to a wholly paternalistic society, in which all decisions are made for us by those who claim to be most capable of determining what is in our best interest. Therefore, by allowing the cancer victim to choose the use of Laetrile, we serve both the right of the adult to follow his own choice and the best interest of society in the long run.

It is clear that the question of autonomy vs. paternalism needs to be resolved if we are to decide between the social policy embodied in the Food and Drug Act and that embodied in the Indiana state statute. In the next two chapters we will see what utilitarianism and deontology have to say about this issue.

12·4 LICENSING REQUIREMENTS

In every state in the United States it is illegal to practice medicine without a license. Furthermore, this license can only be obtained by those who have completed the required course of study and internship at an accredited medical school and an approved hospital and who have then passed the relevant exams. While we are all aware of these licensing requirements, few of us have given much thought to the justification of such a system. In this section, we will see how the mere existence of a licensing system gives rise to our fundamental questions about autonomy and paternalism.

In medieval times, western Europe was dominated by the *guild system*, a network of merchant and trade associations which served to maintain standards and protect the members' interests. Many trades could be practiced only by members of the appropriate guild. But the rise of modern society brought, along with many other changes, the abolishment of the guild system. Eventually, one did not need to belong to a guild in order to practice his trade or profession. Yet our present-day licensing system is in many ways analogous to the medieval guild system.

Another observation which alerts us to the need to reconsider the justifications for a licensing system is the growing number of professions which are required to license their practitioners. In addition to requiring the licensing of doctors, lawyers, pharmacists, and psychologists, there are state laws and municipal ordinances that, in certain localities, call for the licensing of barbers, dealers in scrap tobacco, tree surgeons, guide dog trainers, and hypertrichologists (people who remove excessive and unsightly hair). Moreover, the licensing board of a particular trade or profession is, as a rule, directly controlled by those who practice that trade or profession. These observations should make us think twice about the matter of licensing.

In many studies which have been conducted to determine the effects of licensing, the results often seem to indicate that the main beneficiaries of this system are the licensed professionals themselves. Strict licensing requirements may be used by the professionals to exclude competition and to keep prices artificially high. However, it is not the purpose of this section to focus on these possible abuses of the licensing system. Rather, our concern is with the theoretical justifications for having such a system. These possible abuses have been suggested only for the sake of increasing the reader's awareness that a licensing system should never be taken for granted.

In looking at the question of licensing requirements from a more theoretical perspective, it is important to distinguish three possible types of systems for controlling the practice of medicine.

Registration System. Under this system, anyone who wants to practice medicine could do so simply by listing his name and providing appropriate information about himself in an official register. There would be no prerequisites for listing oneself in the register. The purpose of maintaining such a list would be to ensure that if there were any problems in connection with someone's practice of medicine, the state would know where to find him, what his background was, and so on.

Certification System. Under this system, the government would issue a certificate to those who meet certain requirements. The purpose of certification would be to enable prospective patients to ascertain whether a practitioner had met these requirements. Anyone who wanted to could practice medicine, but only those who had met the stipulated requirements would be able to advertise themselves as certified physicians. In this way, the public would be protected against fraud but would be free to knowingly choose, if they so desired, to be treated by a noncertified medical practitioner.

Licensing System. Under this system, which is the one now in effect, each state issues a license to practice medicine to those who meet certain requirements. No one may practice medicine in a state in which he is not licensed, even if people know he has not met those requirements and wish to be treated by him anyway.

An examination of these three possibilities makes it clear that only the last one raises the question of autonomy vs. paternalism. Those who believe that society must always respect the autonomous choices of adults would not object to the registration or certification systems, because they both allow anyone who so desires to practice medicine, and they also allow all adults to choose, without restriction, whomever they want as their medical practitioner. Only licensing requirements raise a problem for autonomy, for they dictate — even if two adults come to a free agreement, without fraud or coercion—which persons may provide medical treatment and which may not. So those who believe in an adult's right to make unrestricted autonomous decisions must at least question the legitimacy of licensing requirements.

Those who defend licensing requirements see things differently. They question why someone would choose to be treated by a practitioner who has not met the requirements necessary to obtain a license. The most probable explanations are either that the person is seeking an unorthodox type of medical treatment or that he is being offered medical services at cut-rate prices. Unorthodox and/or unusually cheap treatments appeal primarily to people who are uneducated or unable, because of their illness, to exercise sound judgment. If these people are allowed to make autonomous medical decisions, they could unwittingly jeopardize their lives. So, for their own benefit, society must insist that they be treated only by qualified, licensed physicians.

Here we have seen a clear expression of a paternalistic argument. It stands in marked contrast to the argument that would, at most, permit a certification system for controlling the practice of medicine. We shall be looking at these issues more fully as we examine them in the next two chapters, first from the utilitarian perspective and then from the deontological point of view.

12·5 INVOLUNTARY CIVIL CONFINEMENT

Our final example of an area in which medical practice gives rise to the problem of autonomy vs. paternalism is that of involuntary civil confinement in a mental institution, where the person is confined because he is viewed as a threat to himself rather than to others. The legal and moral questions that arise in this context are quite complex, so we need to examine them with great care. To begin, let us distinguish four rationales for confining someone in a mental institution.

Confinement of the Criminally Insane.   In our society, as in most advanced societies, insanity is a legally recognized excuse against criminal charges. We saw in Chapter 3 that an *excuse* is an argument designed to show that the defendant should not be punished even though he has committed the crime in question. The insanity excuse claims that the defendant should not be punished for the crime with which he has been charged because his mental illness makes him not responsible for his actions, in particular, for committing that crime. Although we recognize this excuse, we do not, where it is employed successfully, simply let the criminal go free. In most jurisdictions, he is automatically (or at least usually) confined against his will in an institution for the treatment of the mentally ill until such time as he is certified as sane.

This type of confinement, in which the criminal is confined against his will, raises some problems. In many cases, the insane criminal winds up spending more time confined in a mental institution than he would have spent in jail had he been punished for his crime. Furthermore, confinement in a mental institution often turns out to be a much worse punishment than the criminal would have received had he been punished for his crime. While these are serious value questions concerning confinement of the criminally insane, they are not questions of paternalism vs. autonomy, so we will not pursue them here.

Voluntary Confinement of Those Who Are Mentally Ill. There are many people who, in seeking help for their problems, voluntarily commit themselves to confinement in a mental institution. These cases, because they involve the autonomous choice of the person who is confined, also do not raise any questions of autonomy vs. paternalism.

Involuntary Civil Confinement of Those Who Are a Threat to Society. Some people are involuntarily confined in mental institutions not because they have committed a crime but because they have been judged as potentially dangerous to society. This type of involuntary confinement raises many important questions. There is, to begin with, the very difficult question of the reliability of our predictions. How likely must it be that the person will harm others before we should confine him against his will? And how reliable are our estimates of this likelihood? Moreover, given that the person has not yet harmed anyone, are we really justified in confining him? Is this a case of punishment before a crime, or is it rather like the case of putting someone with an infectious disease into quarantine to protect the rest of us from being infected? Again, although these are important problems for society, we will disregard this rationale for confinement and its attendant problems for now, because they do not raise our issue of autonomy vs. paternalism. That is, if we do choose to confine someone against his will, we are doing so for our benefit, to protect ourselves, not for his benefit. So if we make that choice, it is not a paternalistic choice. Therefore, the value problems this type of case raises are questions of individual autonomy vs. protection of society, not questions of individual autonomy vs. paternalism.

Involuntary Civil Confinement to Protect the Individual from Harming Himself. It is this rationale for confinement, and only this one, which gives rise to the problem of autonomy vs. paternalism. In such cases, the person does not wish to be confined; his autonomous choice is to remain free. If we believe in respecting autonomous choices, then we must oppose such involuntary commitment. On the other hand, if we do accept this type of involuntary commitment, we do so because we believe it is for the best interest of the person being confined. We are confining him in order to protect him from himself. Acceptance of this rationale presupposes a belief in a form of paternalism, at least in regard to the person in question.

One of the most common reasons for this type of confinement is to prevent a suicidal person from killing himself. Those who are willing to accept paternalism in such a case must believe that preventing someone from taking his own life takes priority over respecting that person's desires and his freely made decisions. Conversely, those who refuse to accept this form of involuntary confinement must be committed to the view that respecting an individual's right to be autonomous takes priority over society's duty to try to save his life.

One point must be made clear. Many of those who oppose this type of involuntary civil confinement do so either because they are concerned that our mental institutions make no real effort to help these unfortunate people or because they are concerned with abuses. The latter concern is the fear that some families or communities may use this rationale for confinement as an excuse for getting rid of unwanted burdens. Unfortunately, there are cases in which this system of involuntary civil confinement actually has been abused in this way. And adding to this tragic situation is the fact that even when the person really does need help, there is often no help available in the institutions in which he is confined.

These are important points, and there is no doubt that they play some role in shaping the way we view these issues. But they are not pertinent to our discussion, so we will put them aside. Instead, let us imagine that society has strengthened its procedural safeguards so that the possibility of abuse is mimimized and that these institutions are truly capable of helping those who are committed to them. Now we are left with the fundamental value question of whether society still has a right to adopt a paternalistic stance toward these people. Should we decide for them that they are better off confined, even when they pose no threat to us? In the succeeding chapters, we will see how the utilitarian and deontological perspectives on autonomy and paternalism view this fundamental value question.

Exercises

Define in your own words the following terms:

1. paternalistic decision making
2. autonomous decision making

3. guild system
4. Indiana/FDA statutory distinction
5. registration/certification/licensing systems distinction
6. confinement of criminally insane
7. involuntary civil confinement
8. threat to self/threat to others distinction

Review Questions

1. What are the major reasons offered for extending paternalistic decision making from children to adults?
2. What are the arguments for and against allowing Jehovah's Witnesses to refuse emergency blood transfusions?
3. What are the major arguments for and against the right to die with dignity? How do they differ from the arguments in Question 2?
4. How does the Indiana drug control scheme differ from the federal scheme? What are the strengths and weaknesses of each scheme?
5. In what ways, if any, are licensing requirements like the old guild system?
6. What are the advantages and disadvantages of registration, certification, and licensing?
7. What are the different conditions under which society confines insane people? What are the main value questions which arise in each of these conditions?
8. In what way does involuntary civil confinement of those not a threat to others raise the question of the legitimacy of paternalism?

Questions for Further Thought

1. What limitations, if any, should be imposed upon the types of choices that adults can make for children even in those cases in which paternalistic decision making is clearly justified? How should these limitations be enforced without unduly interfering with the parent-child relationship?
2. Comment on the following statement: "No one can really freely choose, with appropriate knowledge, to use a drug like Laetrile. All such instances are really just cases of indirect fraud and coercion on the part of those peddling such drugs."
3. What principle would you use to distinguish those professions which we probably should certify and/or license from those which we should not bother to certify and/or license? Give examples of each type.
4. How, if at all, should we distinguish the confinement of the criminally insane from the confinement of the criminal? Should their

treatment be different? Should their civil rights be different? Should the duration of their stay be different?

5. On what basis would you distinguish involuntary civil confinement of those who are considered a threat to society from punishment that takes place before a crime is committed? By the treatment of those confined? By their rights? By the duration of their confinement? Or. . . . ?

Chapter Thirteen

Autonomy and Paternalism: A Utilitarian Perspective

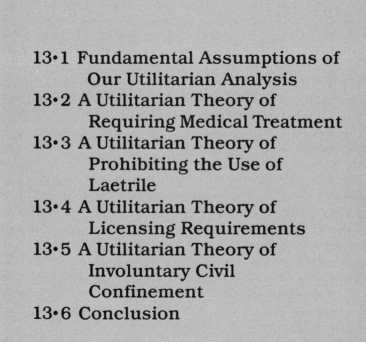

13·1 FUNDAMENTAL ASSUMPTIONS OF OUR UTILITARIAN ANALYSIS

The issue of paternalism vs. autonomy is really a debate over who should make which decisions for whom. At first glance, this debate is not one which easily fits into the utilitarian perspective. After all, utilitarians are concerned exclusively with the question, What will produce the best results? Thus, it would seem that, in any particular case, the utilitarian should be concerned not with who makes the decision but with which decision is made. In other words, we expect the utilitarian to be primarily concerned with ensuring that we follow the decision which will produce the best results for all those affected. We do not expect him to worry very much over whose decision it is.

To illustrate, consider, for example, the previous chapter's case of the involuntary civil confinement of someone who is judged to be a threat to himself. We might expect the utilitarian's sole concern here to be that of considering the consequences of committing or failing to commit the person in question. If the consequences are good, he should be committed; if they are bad, he should not be committed. We would not expect the utilitarian to care one way or the other who makes this judgment.

One thing the utilitarian certainly is not concerned about is the *rights* of adults to be autonomous decision makers. There are many people who are concerned with who makes the decisions, as well as with what decisions are made, because they believe that people have certain rights to make decisions about their own lives. But utilitarians are not among these analysts. As we have seen many times in this book, utilitarians do not believe in rights as independent moral considerations. Because this is so, they cannot appeal to the rights of autonomous decision makers as a way of explaining why they are concerned with who makes the decision as well as with what decision is made.

There are two major themes which utilitarians develop to help explain their reasons for being concerned not only with what decision is made but also with who makes the decision. One has to do with the relative competency of various decision makers and the other has to do with the desires people have to be autonomous decision makers. Let's look at each of these separately.

As a society, we have neither the time nor the means to examine all the decisions made by everyone in order to determine whether each decision is likely to lead to the best consequences. It is ludicrous even to consider such an undertaking. We need, therefore, to have some general guidelines as to whose decisions we want to check in which contexts and whose decisions we want to allow to be carried out without checking. Since we have little trust in children's ability to make important decisions, we want someone else (usually their parents) either to make those decisions for them or at least to check on them. Since we have little trust in the decisions made by private people that have tremendous impact on the lives of others, we want to institute a variety of mechanisms for checking and, if necessary, correcting those decisions. However, in cases in which an adult makes a decision whose primary impact is upon himself, it makes sense from a utilitarian point of view to allow that decision to go unchecked and to stand without any social control. To begin with, the individual is probably the best judge of which action will be best for him. Moreover, these actions have little, if any, impact upon the rest of us, and the cost of trying to oversee the individual's decisions would probably be much greater than any benefits that might accrue. Therefore, except in special cases, we have utilitarian reasons for respecting autonomous decision making.

The second way in which utilitarians address the question of who makes which decisions is in terms of people's desire to control their own lives and to be autonomous decision makers. This desire, like all others, is one which the utilitarian has to take into account. Even if we think that the person is making the wrong decision, because the consequences to him would not be good, we might still have good utilitarian reasons for allowing him to carry out his own decisions. If the person in question is like most of us, he will have a great desire to make his own decisions and be the master of his own fate. The frustration of desire that occurs when we overrule his decision and act paternalistically toward him will often outweigh any benefits that he might gain from the decisions we make for him. In this way, without referring to any rights of autonomy, the utilitarian can ascribe independent importance to allowing adults to be autonomous decision makers.

None of this is to imply that the utilitarian always believes in autonomy. These arguments simply show that there are good utilitarian reasons for respecting people's autonomous choices. From previous chapters, we know that this means that there can also be good utilitarian reasons that outweigh these considerations and which call upon us to behave paternalistically. For instance, if the consequences to the person of following his own choice are very bad, then we may be compelled to overrule his choice and behave paternalistically toward him. The utilitarian, in this area as in others, tells us that we must weigh these consequences. But we have seen that while some consequences result directly from the decision that is made, others are the result of who makes the decision. In the remaining sections of this chapter, we shall see how the utilitarian applies his basic framework to the questions we raised in Chapter 12.

13·2 A UTILITARIAN THEORY OF REQUIRING MEDICAL TREATMENT

In light of the utilitarian analysis developed in the previous section, we are now in a position to examine the questions raised in Chapter 12. The first of the questions we will consider is that of the conditions under which we may justifiably require someone to have medical treatment against his will. Continuing with the examples from section 12.2, we will look at this question in terms of the Jehovah's Witness who refuses a blood transfusion and the terminally ill patient who refuses life-saving treatment.

It is worth reiterating that there are several familiar arguments to which the utilitarian thinker *cannot* appeal in dealing with these cases. He cannot appeal to the individual's right to make autonomous decisions, because utilitarians do not view human rights as independent moral considerations. For this reason, he also cannot appeal to the individual's right to religious freedom, which many judges have citied in their arguments in favor of autonomy in Jehovah's Witnesses' cases. Instead, the utilitarian appeals to the consequences of respecting or opposing the individual's wishes in each situation. Let us look at each of our cases separately.

In the case of the terminally ill patient who wishes to die earlier with dignity rather than later without it, the utilitarian approach is quite straightforward. We simply need to ascertain the consequences of insisting upon saving the person. To begin with, he will have to suffer the pain and indignity that he wants to avoid. Moreover, we may impose a great personal and financial burden on his family. Finally, he will have to bear the frustration of having his wishes ignored and his desire to die with dignity thwarted. In all, there are several substantial losses that result from a paternalistic decision to disregard the person's wishes.

It is harder to see the gains that might result from this paternalistic decision. Some people claim that there is a gain to the doctors and the hospitals. These institutions, they argue, are devoted to the preservation of life, and by thwarting this endeavor, we undermine their purpose and diminish their stature. There is, therefore, some *social gain* in allowing the struggle to save life to continue even against the wishes of the patient. Those who oppose this claim assert that even if these benefits exist, it is difficult to believe that they outweigh the substantial losses to the individual. Moreover, it is not clear whether we really want to encourage these institutions to maintain as their monolithic goal the preservation of life at any cost. If this utilitarian analysis is right, we may well want to encourage a different attitude in which physicians and hospitals come to see their role as aids to the patient, helping to keep him alive when the reward of life is worth the struggle, but helping him to die with dignity when that is his reasonable choice. In sum, the utilitarian analysis clearly leads to the conclusion that in this case the best consequences will result from the person being allowed to refuse medical treatment.

The issue is much more complicated in the case of the Jehovah's Witness. Here, the patient wishes to refuse medical treatment because he believes that he will go to hell if he has a blood transfusion. People who do not accept this belief as reasonable may think that this person's judgment is a bad one because it is based on an erroneous theological belief. They would thus conclude that he, like most other human beings, will be better off if his life is saved. At first glance, then, the utilitarian point of view would seem to suggest that society should intervene in a paternalistic fashion here, because paternalism will lead to better consequences in this sort of case than will the autonomous decisions of the Jehovah's Witness.

On closer examination, however, we see that things are not so simple. To begin with, we have to consider the implications for this person's life of his being forced to have the transfusion. Will he feel guilty because he has been compelled to sin in this way? Will this feeling of guilt be sufficient to cloud the rest of his life? And, if so, is it sufficient to make us conclude that he really would be best off if he were not compelled to have this treatment? It is hard to answer these questions. One of the difficulties is in deciding how likely it is that the person will feel this great sense of guilt and sin and shame, considering that he was treated against his will. Second, we have to ask what the cost is to society of infringing on the religious beliefs of this adult. Will this infringement lead to a widespread feeling that religious beliefs in general are open to being violated by those in society who do not necessarily share them? If so, is this consequence sufficiently bad to outweigh the benefits that accrue from saving the person's life?

We cannot attempt to settle these issues here. All that we shall conclude is that the case of the Jehovah's Witness is much more complicated than the case of the person who wishes to die with dignity. In the latter, despite the lack of a belief in individual rights, the utilitarian is almost certain to agree that the person's wishes to die with dignity should be respected. In the former, while there is a powerful utilitarian argument for disregarding the wishes of the person and saving him, even if this means giving him a blood transfusion, this case needs to be thought through much more fully, for there are considerations which suggest otherwise. As we might expect, the utilitarian sides neither completely with autonomy nor completely with paternalism.

13·3 A UTILITARIAN THEORY OF PROHIBITING THE USE OF LAETRILE

The question of prohibiting the use of Laetrile is not an independent question about the use of just that drug. There is, after all, no special law banning the use of Laetrile. The relevant statute is the 1962 amendments to the Pure Food and Drug Act, which require that no drug can be manufactured, distributed, prescribed, and used until it has proved to be both safe and effective. The question that we have to consider, then, is whether this form of paternalistic legislation is desirable from a utilitarian perspective, and, if so, whether the use of Laetrile should be made an exception.

To sharpen the focus of these questions, it is helpful to imagine what an alternative scheme might be like. One that immediately suggests itself is that which the state of Indiana has adopted for dealing with Laetrile. On this model, no absolute ban is imposed on the use of any drug unless there is evidence that it is harmful. Instead, all those who manufacture, distribute, or prescribe the drug are simply required to inform prospective users of the recognized opinion concerning the drug's effectiveness. Such a statute provides ample protection against fraud while still allowing freedom of choice for the patient.

This type of scheme can easily be justified from a utilitarian point of view, since the consequences of adopting it are clearly positive. For one thing, it is difficult for ordinary citizens to know whether a course of treatment involving the use of certain drugs is desirable, because most people do not have access to the relevant information nor the training to fully evaluate the issues. Consequently, they are vulnerable to fraudulent advertising of worthless drugs. The results of this fraud are very bad, in part because of the great deal of money that is spent on the worthless drugs, and in part because of the risk to people's health that comes directly from using the wrong drugs and indirectly from not using the drugs that could help them. Our major question, then, is whether there are any utilitarian reasons for requiring that drugs be proven safe and effective before they can be used (as we now require) or whether we would be better off requiring simply that users of any drug be provided with the type of information set forth in the Indiana statute.

There is one obvious reason, from the utilitarian point of view, for preferring a scheme like the Indiana statute, which emphasizes freedom of choice. The reason is that whenever we prohibit people from using whatever drugs they want to treat their illnesses, we frustrate their strongly felt desires to use those drugs. After all, people do have a strong desire to make decisions for themselves and to determine the course of their lives, and statutes like the Pure Food and Drug Act can frustrate that desire. So we must begin our comparison of the two statutory approaches with the recognition that, from the utilitarian point of view, there is a substantial objection to the current Pure Food and Drug Act.

There is, nevertheless, a powerful utilitarian defense of the current statute. History has shown that people who are very sick are also very gullible. In their desire to get well, and out of their fears of prolonged illness and death, they are often willing to try any remedy that presents itself, even those that have been judged totally worthless by standard medical opinion. It is interesting to speculate on the rationale behind these decisions. Part of it no doubt reflects a tension between the patient and the physician. In many cases, patients come to view the physician as an enemy rather than a helper; as a result, they think the physician is deliberately withholding the untested and unproven medicines. Another factor may simply be a loss of faith in traditional medicine. But whatever the rationale, there is no doubt that many people will choose the worthless remedy over the treatment that could really help them. If this is true now, when worthless remedies are sold in violation of the law, it would likely be even more true if we did not have a statute like the Pure Food and Drug Act. As a result of not having such a law, many people would suffer severe illness or death because they would forsake the medical treatment which could help them and turn instead to worthless remedies. These unfortunate consequences should outweigh the beneficial consequences of allowing people to choose their own treatment. In short, then, it seems as though the utilitarian would have to be supportive of the current paternalistic statutes.

There is, however, one further complication. The heart of the argument above was that the current statutes are desirable because they channel people toward effective medical treatment and away from worthless remedies. Suppose, however, that we are dealing with a case in which there are no recognized remedies. Suppose we are dealing with a patient for whom orthodox medical science has nothing to offer except pain-killing drugs to lessen the pain of dying. Some of the people who wish to use Laetrile are precisely in this situation. And one or two courts (whose opinions have been overruled) have wanted to say that such people should be entitled to use whatever medicines they believe can help them. These courts have couched their decisions in terms of the rights of that individual patient. Such a claim is not, of course, acceptable from the utilitarian point of view. Still, their point can be formulated within the utilitarian framework. Don't better consequences result from allowing terminal patients to use any remedies they wish? After all, at least there is some satisfaction gained from following one's own desires and beliefs, and from knowing that no stone has been left unturned. Since we cannot help them anyway, what does anyone gain by our stopping them?

Our utilitarian analysis, therefore, approves of the current scheme which prohibits the manufacture, distribution, prescription, and use of any drug that has not been proven safe and effective. But it suggests that we may want to build into this scheme, if we can, an exception for those whom we cannot help by orthodox means.

13·4 A UTILITARIAN THEORY OF LICENSING REQUIREMENTS

In section 12.4 we saw that a crucial social choice is that between a system of *certifying* medical practitioners and one of *licensing* medical practitioners. In each system the government issues a certificate to those who have met certain requirements. The crucial difference is that under the certification system anyone who wants to can practice medicine but only those who have met the stipulated requirements are able to advertise themselves as certified physicians, whereas under the licensing system, only those who meet the requirements for certification can practice medicine. Someone who does not meet those requirements is not allowed to practice medicine, even if his potential patients know that he does not meet the requirements and still desire to be treated by him.

There is an important way in which the difference between a certification system and a licensing system closely parallels the difference, discussed in the last section, between the Indiana Laetrile scheme for controlling the use of medicines and the current Pure Food and Drug Act scheme for controlling the use of medicines. The Indiana scheme and the scheme for certifying physicians both ensure that prospective patients will have certain information—namely, about the proven effectiveness of medicines and about the training of possible physicians—and then leave the final decision up to the individual patient. Anyone who so desires may use unproven drugs and uncertified physicians. Conversely, both the Pure Food and Drug Act scheme and the scheme for licensing physicians leave the patient no choice in these matters. He may not use an uncertified physician and he may not use unproven drugs. His freedom of choice is in that way limited. In short, the licensing of physicians and the Pure Food and Drug Act are examples of paternalistic schemes in which the state makes decisions for the good of the individual. The certifying of physicians and the Indiana system for controlling the use of Laetrile are examples of schemes for leaving decision making in the hands of individuals.

This parallel suggests that some of the arguments offered in the previous section can be carried over to this discussion. For example, medical licensing schemes, like the Pure Food and Drug Act, have the unfortunate consequence of frustrating people's strong desires to make decisions for themselves and to determine the course of their own lives. Patients who wish to use noncertified medical practitioners and who are not allowed to do so are just as frustrated by this limitation of their autonomy as are patients who want to use unproven medicines. By the same token, just as there are powerful utilitarian reasons for approving laws like the Pure Food and Drug Act, there are similarly powerful reasons for approving the licensing of physicians. Without such laws, many people will choose incompetent practitioners rather than competent, certified physicians. The result may be severe illness or death. If, however, we have laws preventing incompetent people from practicing medicine, then we significantly reduce the number of unnecessary deaths and illnesses.

All this might suggest that we should simply apply our analysis of the previous section and conclude that utilitarians should approve of licensing schemes in much the same way they approve of the current Pure Food and Drug Act. We should not, however, be misled by this seemingly close parallel. There is an important difference between these cases. While utilitarians may well conclude that people should not be allowed to use untested drugs, it is not clear that they would advocate the licensing of physicians. Let's look at the reasons behind this distinction.

Licensing requirements typically impose very high standards. This is certainly true for medical practitioners, who must go through a long and expensive training period. In recompense, they are well paid for the medical care they provide. Because of the substantial fees charged by these highly skilled professionals, it may well make sense, at least for uncomplicated illnesses, to see medical practitioners who are less well trained and who charge correspondingly lower fees. When society prohibits that option by imposing strict licensing laws, the health of many people of modest means may suffer. For that reason, the licensing laws, at least as they are normally formulated, may not lead to as good consequences as would a system of certification.

Let's put this point another way. The utilitarian judgment that we ought to prohibit people who can be helped by orthodox medical techniques from using untested drugs is based on the belief that the best consequences for those people will result from overruling their misguided decisions to use such drugs. In the case of using unlicensed physicians, however, it is not clear that their judgment is really mistaken. Perhaps it would be best if we were to certify medical practitioners at varying levels of expertise, and then people could choose among these practitioners based on their needs and on the amount they are willing to spend. We may, perhaps, retain some sort of licensing system in that we would prohibit those with no expertise from practicing medicine. With this one aspect of licensing retained, utilitarians might do best to move over to this *differential certification scheme.* In short, utilitarians might, despite the seemingly plausible parallels we saw initially, distinguish between the drug control scheme envisaged under the Pure Food and Drug Act and our current scheme for licensing physicians, approving the former while questioning the latter.

13·5 A UTILITARIAN THEORY OF INVOLUNTARY CIVIL CONFINEMENT

The final area in which we shall examine the utilitarian perspective on the conflict between autonomy and paternalism is that of involuntary civil confinement. As we saw in section 12.5, this type of confinement must be distinguished from the confinement of the criminally insane, from the voluntary confinement of those who are mentally ill, and from the involuntary civil confinement of those who are a threat to society. Only the involuntary confinement of those who are perceived as a threat to themselves raises the question of autonomy vs. paternalism.

Many utilitarian thinkers find it easy to argue that the consequences of having a system of involuntary civil confinement for those who are merely harmful to themselves are so bad that we should do away with that system entirely. These consequences involve the use of the system, by some families, as a way to confine those whom they want to get rid of, and the extremely low quality of care available to those who might legitimately be confined. Nevertheless, as we pointed out in section 12.5, these consequences detract from the purpose of our discussion, so we shall put them aside and suppose that we could strengthen our procedural safeguards to avoid abuse and improve the quality of care these institutions provide. Now what do utilitarians say to this form of confinement?

With these consequences supposed away, utilitarians no longer find an easy answer to this question. After all, there will undoubtedly be cases of this type of involuntary civil confinement in which the consequences will be good and other cases in which the consequences will be bad. The best we can do, therefore, is to look at how the utilitarian approaches some specific cases.

The first case is that of the suicidal person whom we are involuntarily confining to prevent him from killing himself. In understanding the utilitarian analysis of such cases, it is helpful to recall an earlier discussion, in section 10.2, where we saw that utilitarians believe that suicide is the morally desirable response to situations in which the consequences of the person's continuing to exist are worse than the consequences of his staying alive. With this in mind, it is hard to see what sort of argument the utilitarian can make in favor of confining someone against his will in order to prevent him from committing suicide. If the consequences of his committing suicide are better than the consequences of his staying alive, then surely the consequences of institutionalizing him to ensure that he stays alive are worse than the consequences of leaving him free to commit suicide.

There are, however, many cases in which the suicidal person would be better off staying alive. Here, utilitarians believe that committing suicide is morally wrong. Moreover, in such cases we would be right to confine the person involuntarily to prevent him from committing suicide, for the consequences of keeping him alive — even in an institution — are better than the consequences of letting him die. So, as usual, the utilitarian will want to look at each case individually. He will evaluate the consequences of that person staying alive and of his dying, and use that evaluation as the major criterion for deciding whether or not to confine the person to prevent him from committing suicide.

The second case which we will examine is that of the person who is a threat to himself not because he is likely to harm or kill himself, but because he is incapable of taking care of himself. Consider, for example, the following true story. Some time ago, a man spent 52 days and nights in a shabby bus shelter on Detroit's West Side. Living on handouts from a nearby hamburger stand, but refusing offers of a warm place to sleep, he spent the nights on the shelter's wooden bench, pulling a thin raincoat over his head for protection against the cold winds that shook the structure. Most of the time he just sat with head bowed, staring at the litter piled around his feet by the wind. What shall we do with this unfortunate person who clearly cannot make any decisions for himself?

The utilitarian will find it much easier to justify involuntary civil confinement in this type of situation. Unlike many potential suicide cases, in this case there is every reason to suppose that our judgment of what would produce the best consequences for this person is better than the individual's own judgment. Thus, the utilitarian will have little difficulty in justifying paternalism.

Although we have looked at only two of the many cases for which society practices involuntary civil confinement to protect people from themselves, it should be clear that the utilitarian will always have to judge the morality of this issue independently for each case.

13•6 CONCLUSION

Utilitarianism, as we have seen, approaches the question of autonomy vs. paternalism by determining what pattern of decision making will lead to the best consequences. Sometimes this utilitarian approach leads us to respect the individual's autonomous decisions, particularly when his desire to make his own decision is intense and/or when we have good reason to believe that he is the best judge of what is best for him. Thus, utilitarians will often argue for society to respect people's decisions to terminate medical treatment or to commit suicide. Other times, particularly in those cases where we have little reason to trust the individual's own judgment, utilitarians will argue for society to behave paternalistically to protect people from themselves. For this reason, utilitarians will support the Pure Food and Drug Act, many forms of involuntary civil confinement, and the requirement that Jehovah's Witnesses submit to life-saving medical treatment in violation of their religious tenets. How do these conclusions differ from those based on an analysis of the issues from a deontological perspective? We will see in the next chapter, where we focus on autonomy vs. paternalism in terms of individual rights.

Exercises

Define in your own words the following terms:

1. desire for autonomy
2. social gain from the struggle to save life
3. differential certification scheme
4. involuntary confinement for inability to care for oneself

Review Questions

1. How do utilitarians take into account the question of who is making the decision? Why don't they appeal to the right of autonomy?
2. Under what conditions would utilitarians disregard questions of autonomy?
3. Why would utilitarians be inclined to disregard the wishes of Jehovah's Witnesses and require transfusions? What would lead them to reconsider this conclusion?
4. How would utilitarians defend the Pure Food and Drug Act scheme for controlling drug use? What exceptions might they make?
5. What are the utilitarian arguments for a licensing scheme? What are the utilitarian arguments for something weaker?
6. On what bases will utilitarians decide on the involuntary civil confinement of suicidal patients?

7. In terms of the story of the man in the bus shelter, illustrate how utilitarians would analyze other cases of involuntary confinement.

Questions for Further Thought

1. Utilitarians generally assume that individuals are probably the best judges of what is best for them. In light of the countless examples of disastrous choices that people make, how can that assumption be defended?

2. Consider the possibility that the Jehovah's Witness case and others like it might indeed promote a widespread feeling among religious people that their beliefs may be violated by members of society who do not share them. If this is true, should we view this bad consequence as pertaining only to "respectable" religious groups, or should we consider it a valid utilitarian argument for respecting the autonomous decisions of members of *all* religious sects, including the highly unorthodox cults?

3. What sorts of arguments could be mounted for banning the use of drugs such as Laetrile even when there are no recognized remedies? If we make an exception in these cases, might that lead to worse results than allowing for no exceptions?

4. This chapter's utilitarian argument for certifying rather than licensing doctors rests upon the very high standards that licensing imposes. Should a utilitarian then support licensing schemes with lower standards?

5. What are the procedural safeguards and institutional improvements required by any defensible scheme of involuntary civil confinement?

Chapter Fourteen

Autonomy and Paternalism: A Deontological Perspective

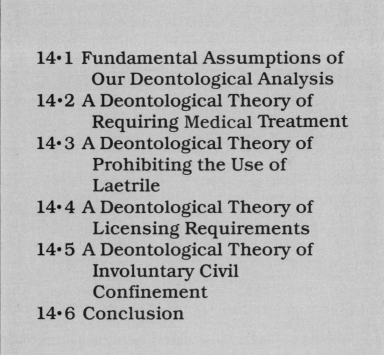

14·1 FUNDAMENTAL ASSUMPTIONS OF OUR DEONTOLOGICAL ANALYSIS

Unlike the utilitarian analysis of the previous chapter, the deontological analysis which we are about to develop is rooted firmly in considerations of individual rights. Several of these rights are central to the questions the deontologist must raise in deciding whether to respect autonomous choices or to impose paternalistic decisions.

One crucial right that plays a role in all our cases is the right of an individual to make and follow his own decisions as long as the resulting actions do not infringe upon the rights of others. Let's see just what is involved here. First, we want to ask, Exactly who is supposed to have this right? We already know that children clearly do not have this right, which is why deontologists have no difficulty in accepting paternalistic behavior toward children. All normal adults clearly do have this right, which is why deontologists typically are strongly supportive of respecting people's autonomous decisions. But what about adults who are suffering from severe mental disorders? And what about adults who do not realize that they lack the knowledge to make reasonable decisions in the areas in question?

Deontologists allow for exceptions by recognizing that people can lose their rights. One way a person can lose his rights is by waiving them. Rights that have been waived cannot be violated. Rights can also be lost, at least to some degree and for some period of time, by infringing upon the rights of others or by threatening to do so. This is why deontologists have no difficulty understanding why a person who is threatening to kill someone may himself be killed if that is the only way to stop him from executing his threat. Neither of these examples, however, can help us with our present analysis. We are not considering cases that involve people who have waived their rights to be autonomous decision makers. Nor are we concerned with cases involving people who have lost their rights as a result of having infringed upon or threatened the rights of others. The deontologist simply views these people, or at least some of them, as having the same status as children: they do not have (or do not have to the full extent) the right to be autonomous decision makers.

There is another right which is important to our deontological analysis. As we explained in section 11.1, the type of deontological theory which we are discussing in this book recognizes that, at least to some degree, people have an obligation to come to the aid of others, even strangers, in times of great need. Furthermore, the obligation to provide aid necessarily implies that people have a right to receive aid. In our present context, this right comes into opposition with the right of people to be autonomous decision makers. For example, if someone is planning to act in a way which poses a great threat to his life or well-being, we may have an obligation to intervene in order to protect him from himself, even if the threat results from his own autonomous decision.

Our obligation to aid people, and their corresponding right to that aid, raises many difficult questions in our analysis of individual cases of paternalism vs. autonomy. Deontologists will sometimes want to say that this sort of obligation leads us to behave paternalistically toward some adults, even if this means infringing upon their rights to autonomy. But if they don't want us to aid them, if they want us to let them alone to carry out their own wishes, haven't they waived their rights to be aided? And haven't we therefore lost our obligation to aid them? In short, can this obligation really be a valid deontological justification for paternalistic action? If it is, it will have to be because the deontologist has decided that the person in question cannot waive his rights and therefore cannot free us from our obligation. But under what conditions will that be the case?

As we examine our issues from a deontological perspective, we will find that these conflicts are integral to the analysis. On the one hand, the obligation to respect an adult's autonomous decisions and to allow him to carry them out is a powerful deontological reason against behaving paternalistically. On the other hand, the obligation to come to the aid of others in times of great need is a powerful deontological reason for behaving paternalistically. Complicating this conflict between our two obligations is the additional need to decide whether, in each given situation, the people in question should have the same rights that normal adults do. The deontologist must consider all these factors in seeking answers to each of our moral problems of paternalism vs. autonomy.

14·2 A DEONTOLOGICAL THEORY OF REQUIRING MEDICAL TREATMENT

In light of the deontological analysis developed in the previous section, we can now examine the questions raised in Chapter 12. The first of the questions we shall consider is that of determining the conditions under which we may justifiably require someone to have medical treatment against his wishes. Following the outline of our discussion in section 12.2, we will focus on two sorts of cases—one involving the Jehovah's Witness, and the other involving the person who wishes to die with dignity.

Let's begin by considering the case of the terminally ill patient who refuses heroic life-saving measures in order to die a dignified death. We saw in section 13.2 that the utilitarian had little difficulty in arguing that we should respect the autonomous decision of this patient. The consequences of respecting his wishes seem vastly superior to the consequences of requiring that his treatment be continued. In a similar fashion, the deontologist also has little difficulty with this type of case. After all, the person's right to be an autonomous decision maker is a powerful reason for respecting his decision to terminate medical treatment. Moreover, our obligation to aid people surely does not extend to forcing someone to continue medical treatment when he is going to die soon anyway. In light of the common judgment that this person is likely to be better off if medical treatment is discontinued, continuing medical treatment in this sort of case hardly seems to be any aid at all. In short, the deontologist has little difficulty in deciding that this is one of those cases in which the person's right to be an autonomous decision maker is not in conflict with our obligation to aid him. Therefore, from a deontological point of view, we have every reason to respect the decision to terminate treatment and no particular reason to continue treatment as a form of paternalistic caring.

The case of the Jehovah's Witness is much more complicated from the deontological point of view, much as it was from the utilitarian point of view. Let us, therefore, look at this problem quite carefully.

We begin by assuming there are the usual strong reasons for respecting the person's wishes. That is, we assume the person in question is a mature and competent adult who has chosen, in accordance with his own values, to refuse medical treatment. As a mature, competent adult, his right to be an autonomous decision maker is a powerful reason for us to respect his decision and not force him to be treated. It is very relevant to add that the basis for his decision is his deeply held religious belief that this form of medical treatment is a sin. The choice that he is making is grounded in his fundamental beliefs, and a failure to respect his choice is a severe challenge to his right to be autonomous. In short, the deontologist sees this as another case in which the individual's right to be an autonomous decision maker is a strong reason for respecting his decision.

This last point deserves further emphasis. In each case in which we consider behaving paternalistically toward a mature adult, it is appropriate to ask, What is the basis of the choice we propose to override? In some cases, where the choice seems to be based on a temporary condition, the deontologist may well want to say that the person's right to be an autonomous decision maker is not as important as our obligation to provide aid for him. In other cases, like the Jehovah's Witness, in which the choice seems to be rooted in some very fundamental beliefs, the deontologist might well conclude that the right to be an autonomous decision maker is much greater than our obligation to provide unwanted paternalistic aid. However, this is not to say that choices based upon religious beliefs should be treated specially. It is, rather, to suggest that choices based upon beliefs which are fundamental to the person's life are especially deserving of respect, and that the right to be an autonomous decision maker should seldom be overruled when the choices are based upon such beliefs.

We have seen that in the case of the Jehovah's Witness there are especially strong reasons for respecting the person's right to make an autonomous decision. While there is no doubt that, from our point of view, we would be aiding him by providing him with a blood transfusion, it is also clear that he would waive his right to this aid. Our obligation to provide the treatment is thus much weaker than his right to be an autonomous decision maker.

In short, it would appear that the intuitionist must conclude that we ought to respect the choice of Jehovah's Witnesses to refuse blood transfusions. The right of individuals to make and follow their autonomous decisions is particularly strong in these cases, and our obligation to come to their aid by providing unwanted medical treatment is particularly weak. In coming to this conclusion, the deontologist may find himself in disagreement with the utilitarian. As we saw in section 13.2, a utilitarian analysis may, in some instances, conclude that we should disregard the wishes of the Jehovah's Witness and require the use of a blood transfusion to save his life.

14·3 A DEONTOLOGICAL THEORY OF PROHIBITING THE USE OF LAETRILE

In examining the deontological approach to the question of prohibiting the use of Laetrile, there are two important points from section 13.3's discussion of the utilitarian analysis which we must keep in mind. The first is that our question is really not specifically about Laetrile. Rather, it more generally concerns the desirability of such paternalistic legislation as the 1962 amendments to the Pure Food and Drug Act, which require that no drug can be manufactured, distributed, prescribed, or used until it has been proven safe and effective. The second point is that there are alternative, less paternalistic ways of protecting the public than banning the use of unproven drugs; an example is the Indiana Laetrile statute, which requires only that prospective users be informed of the recognized medical opinion about the efficacy of the drug in question. The issue which we have to consider from the deontological point of view is the respective merits of the current paternalistic legislation and those of the less paternalistic alternative, as represented by the Indiana statute.

In this case, as in all others involving questions of paternalism, the deontologist is concerned with weighing people's right to act as they choose against the obligation on the part of society to aid them, even if the aid is simply to protect them from their own misguided decisions. Let us weigh each of these factors separately.

For the purpose of our discussion, we are assuming, as usual, that the people who choose to use unproven drugs, such as Laetrile, are mature, competent adults who have a right to act upon their own autonomous choices. How much force, then, should we accord to this right in this particular context? There are two deontological reasons for thinking that this right should not be accorded great force here. First, a decision to use an untested drug is not usually based upon a fundamental tenet of the person's belief system. Thus, an interference with this decision will not encroach upon the person's deeply held beliefs or upon his basic approach to life. To be sure, any interference with an individual's autonomous choices is no doubt a serious matter; but it is not, in the case of using untested drugs, as serious as interfering with, say, the Jehovah's Witness's decision to refuse a blood transfusion. Second, the person who chooses to use an unproven drug is often doing so out of fear, anxiety, or even desperation. This is not to say that the person is not competent to make decisions nor that he has no right to be an autonomous decision maker. Rather, it is simply another deontological reason for claiming that this decision is not to be protected and respected as much as are decisions made on the basis of more profound considerations. In short, there are several reasons for supposing that the individual's right to act as an autonomous decision maker is, in this context, not as forceful as it might be in other contexts.

Let's look at these issues from the perspective of the other factor which we have to weigh, our obligation to aid people in times of need. In this context, the people in question are usually ill and in need of medical treatment. If they choose to use untested or unorthodox methods of treatment rather than the established, well-tested methods, they are likely to do themselves great harm. Their health may be severely impaired or they may even die as a result of not receiving treatment that could have saved them. This is surely a case in which our obligation to aid people is to be taken quite seriously. One way to aid them is to eliminate the possibility of making wrong decisions to use untested drugs, thereby guiding them into a more orthodox form of treatment. This is what we do when we enact legislation against the use of untested drugs. Now, to be sure, these people are quite willing to relieve us of our obligation. They want to make their own decision, and they are perfectly willing to waive their right to our aid. Still, when we keep in mind the fears, anxieties, and desperation that promote such a decision, we will not be tempted to give much weight to their willingness to relieve us of our obligation.

In sum, deontologists seem to conclude that our obligation to aid people by protecting them from their mistaken decision to use unproven drugs is a strong obligation because the loss to them if we do not come to their aid is great. On the other hand, their right to follow their own autonomous choices is less serious in these cases, because their decisions are not rooted in their fundamental beliefs but in the fear, anxiety, and desperation that accompanies their illness. It would appear, therefore, that our obligation to aid these people by protecting them from the disastrous consequences of their own decision outweighs their right to autonomous decision making. Therefore, deontologists should support statutes such as the current Pure Food and Drug Act, which are the forms of aid that our society has chosen as ways to protect its citizens.

One final point needs to be made here. The deontologist, like the utilitarian, may well want to make an exception in the case of people for whom orthodox medical science has nothing to offer other than drugs to lessen the pain of dying. Some of the people who wish to use Laetrile are in precisely this situation. Since we cannot guide them into orthodox treatments in order to help save their lives, there does not seem much point to preventing them from using Laetrile. Thus, we should probably make an exception, if we can, for those who cannot be helped by orthodox means.

Here, our deontological analysis agrees with the corresponding utilitarian analysis. Both approaches seem to lead to the conclusion that we ought to prohibit the use of drugs until they are proven safe and effective except, perhaps, for those patients whom we cannot help by orthodox means. It is interesting to note, however, that while the conclusion is the same, the two approaches have arrived there for very different reasons. The utilitarian analysis, as we learned in section 13.3, came to this conclusion because it views the statutory scheme as leading to the best consequences for the people involved. The deontological approach, as we just saw, came to this conclusion because it sees the statutory scheme as the best way for society to fulfill its obligation to aid citizens in this particular time of need and because it regards that obligation as taking precedence over the individual's right to be an autonomous decision maker.

14·4 A DEONTOLOGICAL THEORY OF LICENSING REQUIREMENTS

In this section, as in the last one, we shall again see an instance in which the deontological approach and the utilitarian approach, for their very distinct reasons, arrive at the same conclusion. This time, the issue concerns licensing requirements. And a moment's thought should show us why this shared opinion is not surprising.

We saw in section 13.4 that the issue of licensing requirements is very similar to the issue of schemes for controlling the use of unproven drugs. The licensing question is a choice between a system of certifying medical practitioners, in which anyone can practice medicine but only those who have met the requirements can advertise themselves as certified physicians, and a system of licensing practitioners, in which only those who have met the requirements may practice medicine, regardless of any potential patients who wish to be treated by someone who is unlicensed. The former system merely protects against fraud, while the latter is a paternalistic scheme designed to protect people from their own bad judgment. So the choice is just like that between such statutes as the Indiana Laetrile statute, which are designed to protect us against fraud, and statutes such as the Pure Food and Drug Act, which are meant to protect us from our own misguided decisions to use unproven drugs. It is the similarity between the issues in the last section and those in this section that accounts for the continued agreement between utilitarianism and deontology.

On this issue of certification systems vs. licensing systems, as on all other issues involving questions of paternalism, the deontologist is concerned with weighing the right of the people in question to act as they choose against the obligation on the part of society to aid them even if the aid is simply to protect them from their own mistaken decisions. On the basis of people's rights, there is no question that we should have a certification system, for only under this system will patients have the choice of going to a noncertified physician if they wish. On the basis of society's obligation to aid those who are in need, it seems that we should have a licensing system, for it is this scheme that will protect people against their own mistaken decisions to use uncertified practitioners.

At this piont, it might seem that we should simply carry over the previous section's conclusions about these two factors. Hence, we might judge that a person's right to use an uncertified physician is less forceful than our obligation to come to his aid, since such a decision is not usually based upon any fundamental beliefs the person may hold and it is often based upon feelings of fear and anxiety induced by his illness. Conversely, our obligation to aid people — in this case, by protecting them from their mistaken decisions — seems to be a very strong obligation, since by going to these uncertified physicians and therefore by not being treated by a properly certified physician, the people in question may severely impair their health or even cause their own death. In short, if we compare this topic with the topic of the previous section, we might well be led to the conclusion that we should support the current licensing requirements rather than the alternative certification scheme.

But this conclusion would be wrong, for it would fail to account for a crucial difference between the two cases. The difference is that the decision to use an unlicensed physician, unlike the decision to use untested drugs, may well be based on sound arguments. And the deontologist, like the utilitarian, may find good reasons for respecting it. Let's look at this issue more closely.

When we judge it correct to prohibit people from going to uncertified physicians as a way of helping them, we do so on the belief that the consequences for those people of following their own decision to use an uncertified physician will be very bad. But it is not clear that this is necessarily so. In fact, they may be better off going to an uncertified, less competent medical practitioner whose services they can afford, and thus will use, rather than going to no physician at all, because they do not want to pay the high fees charged by most certified physicians. In this case, rather than helping people by protecting them from their decisions, the current licensing schemes may well be harming some people by depriving them of affordable medical care.

Perhaps it would be best if the deontologist, like the utilitarian, were to advocate a system in which we certified medical practitioners at varying levels of expertise and then allowed people to choose among these practitioners on the basis of their needs and the amount they are willing to pay. We may perhaps retain some of the licensing system in that we would prohibit people with no expertise from practicing medicine. Through this type of system, a person's right to make autonomous decisions would be respected, except when he chooses to use a totally incompetent practitioner. In such a case, deontologists could, for the reasons given above, support the paternalistic prohibition of this choice.

In sum, deontologists may well agree with the utilitarians in approving the drug control scheme envisaged under the Pure Food and Drug Act and in questioning our current scheme for licensing physicians.

14·5 A DEONTOLOGICAL THEORY OF INVOLUNTARY CIVIL CONFINEMENT

The final area in which we shall examine the deontological perspective on the conflict between autonomy and paternalism is that of involuntary civil confinement. As we saw in section 12.5, this type of confinement must be distinguished from the confinement of the criminally insane, from the voluntary confinement of those who are mentally ill, and from the involuntary civil confinement of those who are a threat to society. Only the involuntary civil confinement of those who are perceived as a threat to themselves raises the question of autonomy vs. paternalism.

As in section 12.5, we shall suppose that society has strengthened the procedural safeguards for involuntary civil confinement so that the possibility of abuse is minimized and that these institutions really can help those whom we must confine. Now what do deontologists say about this form of confinement? Utilitarians, as we saw in section 13.5, dealt with this question by looking at the consequences of each case of confinement. Deontologists will not, of course, adopt that approach. Instead, they will ask whether this form of paternalistic treatment can be justified as a way of fulfilling our obligation to aid those who need help in cases where such treatment violates their rights to autonomy. In these cases, as in all other cases, the deontologist is concerned with weighing the right of the people in question to act as they choose against the obligation on the part of society to come to their aid.

Let us begin with the case of the suicidal patient, whom we are confining in order to prevent him from killing himself. As we saw in section 11.2, deontologists find suicide morally permissible on the grounds that the victim, by virtue of his act, has waived his right not to be killed. Nonetheless, that argument for moral permissibility does not settle our question. We still have to decide whether we have an obligation to prevent the person from exercising this morally permissible option, whether we have an obligation to prevent the person from following his morally permissible but ill-considered judgment.

In some cases, it will be relatively easy to decide that we ought to allow the person to commit suicide. One familiar example of such a case is that of the terminally ill patient who wishes to avoid the pain and indignity of a slow death. Deontologists could hardly say in such a case that we should prevent him from committing suicide as a way of helping him, since we have no reason to believe that preventing him from committing suicide *is* helping him. In fact, it is imposing upon him, for no good reason, burdens that he understandably wishes to avoid.

The more difficult cases involving decisions to confine potential suicide victims are those in which we do not agree with the person's judgment that he would be better off dead. From our point of view, involuntary confinement in this case is a way of helping the person, because he will be better off staying alive. Since the loss of a human life is at stake, our obligation to aid the person is considerable. Against this, however, we have to weigh the person's rights as an autonomous decision maker. Which shall take precedence? Much of the answer depends on the mental processes that led the person to the decision to commit suicide. If the decision is based on rational, stable thought processes and rooted in the fundamental beliefs and values held by the person, then his rights as an autonomous decision maker will be very strong and they should probably take precedence over our obligation to aid him (an obligation from which he certainly would release us). If, however, the decision to commit suicide is rooted in feelings of despair over a temporary crisis, then the relative weights look very different. Here, we might well conclude that the person's judgment is misguided, and our obligation to protect him from himself takes precedence over his right to be an autonomous decision maker.

It seems, then, that the deontologist's approach to the involuntary confinement of suicidal individuals will vary in response to the particular case. As we saw in section 13.5, this was also true of the utilitarian's approach to these cases. While the two approaches draw the same conclusion, they will analyze different cases using very different evaluations. The utilitarian will decide between respecting autonomous decisions and behaving paternalistically on the basis of the consequences to the people in question. The deontologist will decide between these behaviors on the basis of his evaluation of the roots of the person's decision to commit suicide.

The deontologist has much less difficulty deciding what to do in the case of the person who is a threat to himself by being incapable of making the decisions required to take care of himself. For example, in the case of the man who stayed in the bus shelter, which we described in section 13.5, the deontologist sees our obligation to render aid as very strong, and the man's right to be an autonomous decision maker as very weak. In fact, according to the deontologist, what we are doing is protecting him not against his own autonomous decisions but rather against the effects of his failure to make any autonomous decisions. In such a case, it is almost meaningless to talk of leaving him to bear the consequences of his own decisions.

Although we have looked at only two of the many cases for which society practices involuntary civil confinement to protect people from themselves, this examination should make it clear how the deontological analysis of such cases differs from the utilitarian analysis.

14·6 CONCLUSION

Deontology, as we have seen, approaches the question of autonomy vs. paternalism by weighing people's rights to be autonomous decision makers against the obligation of society to aid its members. Sometimes this deontological approach will lead us to respect the individual's autonomous decisions, particularly when his decisions are rooted in his fundamental values and are based upon careful reflection. Thus, deontologists will often argue for society to respect people's decisions to terminate medical treatment or to commit suicide. Other times, the deontologist will argue for society to behave paternalistically to protect people from themselves, particularly when the decisions are based on temporary situations and/or irrational considerations. Although these conclusions are often the same as the conclusions based upon the utilitarian analysis, there will be important differences. For example, deontologists, unlike utilitarians, will respect the decision of the Jehovah's Witness to refuse medical treatment involving blood transfusions, even if it results in his death. The different approaches do lead to some different results even in this area, in which there is much agreement between them.

Exercises

Define in your own words the following terms:

1. right to autonomy
2. choice grounded in fundamental belief
3. mature and competent adult

Review Questions

1. What is the fundamental difference between the deontological and utilitarian analyses of the question of paternalism?
2. What major rights are in conflict in cases of autonomy vs. paternalism? How do deontologists weigh these rights?
3. Why are deontologists more sympathetic than utilitarians to the Jehovah's Witness's refusal of blood transfusions?
4. Why would deontologists support the ban on the use of Laetrile? What, if any, exceptions might they make?
5. Why do deontologists agree with utilitarians about licensing schemes?
6. How do deontologists analyze cases involving the involuntary civil confinement of potential suicides? How do they analyze other cases? In what ways does their analysis differ from the utilitarian analysis?

Questions for Further Thought

1. What criteria must the deontologist employ to decide whether someone has lost his right to be an autonomous decision maker?
2. Why is the basis on which a choice is made so important in deciding whether we should respect that choice? How does this relate to deciding whether to respect the person's right to be an autonomous decision maker? What else might we need to weigh?
3. In both our utilitarian and deontological analyses, we paid little attention to the fact that the choice of the Jehovah's Witness was a religiously based choice. In light of the importance of religious freedom, is that a shortcoming of our analyses?
4. Should deontologists make exceptions for people who cannot be helped by orthodox medical treatment? Is there a deontological reason for preventing such people from using Laetrile?
5. What is the difference between a utilitarian who decides to behave paternalistically on the basis of the consequences to the person and a deontologist who decides to behave paternalistically on the basis of the roots of the person's decision? Give several examples in which these approaches might lead to different decisions.

Index

A 2
B 3
C 4
D 5
E 6
F 7
G 8
H 9
I 0
J 1